THE MAGIC OF

GARLIC

NATURE'S #1 HEALING FOOD

BETTER LIFESTYLE SERIES
7210 CARMEL COURT
BOCA RATON, FL 33433

ALSO BY LYNN ALLISON:

1001 Ways to Make Your Life Better

Natural Stress-Busters for the Whole Family

THE MAGIC OF
GARLIC

ॐ ॐ ॐ ॐ

LYNN
ALLISON

COOL HAND COMMUNICATIONS, INC.

Published by:
COOL HAND COMMUNICATIONS, INC.
1098 N.W. Boca Raton Boulevard
Suite #1
Boca Raton, FL 33432

Library of Congress #93-71985
ISBN: 1-56790-098-4

Printed in the United States of America

Book design by Cheryl Nathan
Illustrations by Mark Cantrell

This book is dedicated to all those who seek alternative, natural ways of improving their lives, and to the growers of garlic.

Contents

❧ ❧ ❧ ❧

Acknowledgments

   ਨ   ਨ   ਨ   ਨ

I'd like to thank Dennis Blank, for putting up with all my questions and phone calls; the Fresh Garlic Association for its helpful information; Tony Damiano, an accomplished chef who helped develop some of the garlic recipes and taught me efficient ways of preparing the glorious bulb; Maddie Schindler, who shared her personal health victories with garlic; Jesse and Barney, who patiently put up with my experimentation in garlicky dog food; and of course Jim Vani, my husband, who chopped, minced and inhaled garlic for months as we tested the recipes. Very special thanks to my food editor, Deborah S. Hartz, at the *Sun Sentinel* newspaper in Fort Lauderdale, Florida for teaching me how to improve my cooking skills.

I am grateful to Wakunaga of America (makers of Kyolic, odorless aged garlic extract) for providing information on the healthy aspects of garlic.

Introduction

　ða　　ða　　ða　　ða

A song of praise to garlic...
Opens new doors to its glories...anyone who takes health and food seriously must have it!
　　　　　—Fran White, herbalist

Garlic has always been a part of my life. Perhaps it is due to my Greek heritage (Mediterranean people love to use garlic in their cuisine) or perhaps it's because I simply love the flavor and aroma of this bulb. But now, having researched and written about the amazing healing powers of this glorious plant, I'm even more of a fanatic!

I don't think I've ever cooked a meal that does not include garlic as a preferred flavoring. There's nothing quite as tantalizing as a garlic-laced stew simmering on the stove or the succulent aroma of garlic-enhanced roast meat in the oven.

I grew up with the smell of freshly-peeled garlic cloves scenting the air as my grandmother prepared skordalia, a traditional Greek dish made with lots of the pungent herb. I remember my father mincing dozens of cloves of garlic for my mother's famous bean soup, a delicacy I still prepare for my family—although it never tastes quite as delicious as I remember from my own childhood.

Unfortunately, I can vividly recall when my love of garlic proved socially embarrassing. I was dating a rather staid fellow whose very proper family frowned upon the odoriferous herb.

I had to choose between him and garlic and ... well, you can't take the herb out of the gal, I guess! Bye, bye boyfriend. Seriously, garlic was not the cause of our breakup, although I'm sure garlic breath had something to do with it! But it was a good indicator of the cultural differences between us.

Over the years, however, the rift between garlic and non-garlic lovers has narrowed, thanks to increasing evidence of its healing and health-giving power. Modern scientists have re-discovered the amazing antibiotic powers of garlic and are currently investigating its ability to lower blood cholesterol levels, prevent heart attacks and attack cancer cells. There is even a growing body of research looking into garlic's anti-viral power and its possible effect on the AIDS epidemic. We'll look into these reports and the many folkloric stories about the magical powers of garlic later on.

I believe that garlic-eating ethnic groups are generally healthier than those who frown upon the herb. That's why we use garlic daily in our home and I hope that you, too, will adopt and adapt garlic for your favorite recipes after you've tried some of ours.

How fortunate that I married an Italian gentleman whose love for garlic even exceeds my own! He liberally rubs the salad bowl with a cut clove to give our Caesar salads extra zip. He carefully inserts slivers of garlic into our roasts, and adds crushed garlic to our dogs' food because we both believe in the folkloric tale that garlic repels fleas (as well as vampires!).

Garlic is a most versatile herb, revered by all chefs around the world. An accomplished chef-friend of mine, Tony Damiano, formerly of the famous Russian Tea Room in New York, uses garlic extensively to flavor his illustrious dishes.

"I lost sixty pounds simply by using less fat and more flavor in my cuisine," says Damiano, who now operates his own restaurant, called Damiano's at Tarrimore House in Delray Beach, Florida. "Garlic plays an important role in creating both subtle and assertive flavors in almost any dish you create. And the real beauty of garlic is that it's a team player. Using garlic with other herbs, notably ginger and coriander in Asian cuisine, creates a symphony of flavor."

Perhaps that's why the Chinese have such a low incidence of cancer, and why the prestigious National Institutes of Health has launched a major research project into the cancer-fighting effects of this popular herb. Dr. Carolyn Clifford, chief of the diet and cancer branch, is heading a $20.5 million, five-year study of the possible cancer-fighting benefits of certain foods, including garlic.

Many other researchers, whom we'll mention later, are firmly convinced that garlic helps lower blood cholesterol levels, boosts your immune system and even battles the common cold!

The healing powers of garlic aren't new discoveries, although I'm sure current researchers would like to think they've tripped upon amazing, uncharted scientific territory.

People throughout history believed that garlic warded off a variety of illnesses. There's even an old Welsh rhyme that goes:

"Eat leeks in March and garlic in May
And all year after physicians may play!"

Ancient civilizations often hailed garlic as a regal remedy, worthy of worship. In some countries, garlic was actually used as currency.

It's said that Roman gladiators were instructed to eat garlic to boost their prowess in the stadium; medieval medicine men prescribed garlic for everything from the common cold to curing sexual problems.

Our generation, in its search for holistic ways to stay healthy, is revitalizing garlic as a popular healing food. This flavorful herb has been restored to its rightful throne as the king of designer foods that fight disease.

If you've already jumped on the garlicky wagon, be assured you're not alone in your love for the herb nicknamed "the stinking rose." According to the California-based Fresh Garlic Association, garlic production and its use are on the rise in the United States. Just look at these statistics:

In the 1930s, only 16 million pounds of garlic were grown. By 1953, the production more than doubled to 35 million pounds. In 1979, the U. S. Department of Agriculture statistics showed a boost to 184.6 million pounds and by 1991 that figure reached 250 million pounds! There are dozens of garlic festivals across the country each year that feature entire menus devoted to garlicky delights. There's also a national organization called "Lovers of the Stinking Rose" that exchanges newsletters and new ideas on the glory of garlic.

It would be interesting to note just how many consumers are turning to garlic merely for culinary use or as a means to improve their health. Most of the garlic lovers I've interviewed for this book are very well aware of its potential healing power and consider this aspect very consciously when they use the herb in cooking.

Noel Kamburian, a famous Mediterranean chef, says that garlic is absolutely instrumental in any dish he creates.

"You can't have a song without music," he points out. "Similarly, you can't create great cuisine without garlic. It's in my veins. I believe my mother used garlic in my baby food!"

Kamburian, like many Europeans, firmly believes in the magic of garlic.

"There is no question about it," he says. "I'm a total believer that garlic is good for your blood, your heart and your general sense of well-being."

Many of us, eager to take control of our own health and medical needs, are turning to nature's healers as alternatives to traditional medicines.

Garlic is considered by many to be an efficient but inexpensive medicine that doesn't need a prescription.

That's why I decided to put together this comprehensive manual for those who want to learn more about the glories of garlic. I think you'll find the recipes in this book are great examples of how garlic enhances common food. You'll also find tips on how to select, prepare and store garlic to ensure top quality and flavor.

Thanks to the Fresh Garlic Association, I learned about garlic ice cream, a recipe I'd never try if it weren't for this book and the research involved. It's quite good, actually, and worth the effort, especially for shock value at your next party!

I hope that this book becomes an entertaining and informative companion to both your home health library and your collection of cookbooks. Many of the recipes I feature are traditional family favorites, while others have been foraged from renowned chefs who also believe in the magic of "the stinking rose."

Greet the Garlic Family

Garlic, scientifically named *Allium sativum*, is a member of the lily family and a first cousin to the branch that includes onions, leeks, chives, scallions and shallots. Although there are more than 300 separate strains of this hardy perennial bulb, they all possess the unique flavor and properties we expect from garlic.

Garlic plants have grayish-green leaves which grow to be a foot or two tall. During their bloom period, the plants send up slender stalks which produce delicate flowers in a round, snowy-white head. The tiny, edible bulbs show up among the flowers, and that's the part most of us are familiar with in our cuisine. A single bulb can contain as many as 12 sections called cloves, which are held together in a parchment-like covering.

Because garlic oxidizes readily when it's cut, it is best to use the fresh cloves. Although there are a myriad of garlic-based products on the shelf in our grocery stores, most rely on the use of preservatives for staying power and flavor. The liquid Kyolic, is a notable exception. It's a pure, odorless extract with the same healing power as fresh garlic.

Scientists have identified a wide variety of compounds within garlic. They include:

- carbohydrates
- sterols
- hydrocarbons
- flavonoids
- anthothyacons
- nucleosides
- enzymes
- minerals and others.

❧ ❧ ❧ ❧

This renowned energy-giving and healing food contains sixty-percent water, and each clove has about:

- 1 gram of carbohydrate
- 0.2 grams of protein
- 0.05 grams of fiber
- 0.01 grams of fat

- Vitamin A
- Vitamin B1, some vitamins B2 and B3
- Vitamin C

The Japanese discovered that, in garlic, Vitamin B1 is combined with allicin, the antibiotic part of garlic that is easily absorbed into the bloodstream. This unusual combination may account for garlic's reported ability to prevent cancer of the colon.

Garlic also has a relatively high level of trace minerals including:

- copper
- iron
- zinc
- tin
- calcium

- manganese
- aluminum
- germanium
- selenium

Germanium and selenium have been the prime focus for modern health-care specialists looking for ways to retard the aging process. Selenium supports the activity of antioxidant vitamins C and E.

Many researchers believe that at least part of garlic's healing powers come from the sulfur-sugar component found within its cells. This component is called scordinin and is generally recognized as a restorative healing nutrient.

Calorie-wise, garlic is very low. The range per clove of garlic is between two and seven calories, a bargain for dieters who rely on taste and flavor to boost food palatability.

Historical Notes

An ancient Chinese doctor, Sun Ssu-mo, once wrote:
"A truly good physician first finds out the cause of the illness, and having found that, he first tries to cure it by food. Only when food fails does he prescribe medication."

As early as 3000 B.C., Chinese scholars were singing the praises of garlic as a natural healer for many diseases. It's also mentioned in the earliest of Sanskrit writings. Dioscorides, the great Greek herbalist of the Roman army, called garlic a holy herb because of its use for purification in spiritual ceremonies.

In 1500 B.C., Egyptian physicians listed twenty-two garlic prescriptions for such complaints as headache, throat disorders and physical weakness. Garlic was so valued by the Egyptians that fifteen pounds of it would purchase a healthy male slave!

In fact, legend has it that the builders of the Great Pyramids ate garlic to gain strength. They actually went on strike when deprived of their favorite food. A famous Egyptian physician, Pliny, prescribed garlic recipes against sixty-one maladies including gastrointestinal disorders, animal bites, asthma, rheumatism, hemorrhoids, ulcers, loss of appetite, tumors and consumption.

The Israelites, wandering in the Sinai desert with nothing but manna to keep them from starving, complained bitterly about missing the spices they left behind—most notably "the leeks and the onions and the garlic."

Hippocrates, the father of medicine himself, recommended garlic as a laxative, diuretic and cure for tumors of the uterus. Jean Carper, in her most informative book, *The Food Pharmacy* (Bantam), says that even first-century Indians recommended garlic to prevent heart disease, a connection that's being investigated and confirmed by modern medical experts today.

In the eighth century B.C., garlic was found growing in the garden of the King of Babylon. And in China, sacrificial lambs were seasoned with garlic to make them more acceptable to the nostrils of the gods.

Even the great sages of philosophy praised garlic. The Greek poet Homer was an ardent fan of the pungent bulb and in his day, lovers were encouraged to send garlic to win the hearts of those they romanced!

It's said that the Christian crusaders moved garlic around the European continent and that Marco Polo, the great voyager, is credited for bringing garlic to various parts of the world on his journeys. In fact, in the high courts of many European countries, diners were asked to compose verses singing the praises of garlic, their favorite flavoring.

These are just some of the healing legends that surround glorious garlic throughout the centuries. There are literally thousands of anecdotes and stories, not to mention songs and poems, written about its amazing healing power.

I predict that garlic will regain its rightful place in our kitchens and medicine chests as a revered herb of healing and enhancing our lives.

Myths and Medicine

"Garlic has been used for so long, for so many illnesses, by so many people and is so effective that pages could be devoted to rhapsodizing about its wonders," says herbalist Jeanne Rose.

And so many pages have. As we've noted there is reference to the wonders of garlic in many ancient scriptures, including the Bible and the Talmud, in which garlic was hailed as an aphrodisiac as well as a healer.

Today, you can find dozens of books written not only by garlic lovers like Lloyd J. Harris (arguably the most prolific of the allium advocates), but also by medical and herbal experts who trace and record the proven benefits of the pungent bulb.

Garlic is alleged to cure high blood pressure, rheumatism, loss of appetite, lung problems, toothaches, freckles, snakebite and even baldness! Garlic was often made into poultices to ease the pain of a tooth or earache. It was actually laid on a baby's navel to help tummy upsets and applied to the soles of a patient's feet to soothe sore tootsies.

Many legends claim the pungent odor of garlic could permeate the body's pores and drive out any ailments.

Despite the incredible legions of remedies and myths associated with garlic's amazing healing powers, there seems to be more than a hint of truth to these tales.

"Thousands of years of folklore can't be all wrong, and laboratory analysis has proven that it's true," says Dr. Victor Gurewich, professor of medicine at Tufts University and chairman of the vascular laboratory at St. Elizabeth's Hospital in Boston.

He discovered garlic can reduce serum cholesterol and inhibit blood clotting. Another scientist from India found that feeding his subjects a clove or two of garlic daily lowered their serum cholesterol by as much as ten percent in twenty-five days! Scientists at Loma Linda University in California found that giving their patients Kyolic, the new odorless garlic supplement developed by the Japanese and available in health food stores here in America, helped lower their high blood cholesterol by a full forty-four points in six months.

In his book, *The Miracle of Garlic* (Health Plus), famous anti-aging doctor Paavo Airola, chronicled his travels to Russia where men are notoriously long-living and healthy well over one hundred.

"I observed that Russian doctors regularly advised their patients to eat lots of garlic," he said. "It is not uncommon to see Russians munching on a clove of garlic or onion the way we eat apples."

Onions, by the way, are a first cousin to garlic. Both are members of the allium family which are sulfur-containing amino acids. The Nobel Prize laureate, Dr. Arthur Stoll, recognized the antibiotic and bactericidal effects of garlic by identifying these amino acids as well as the compounds alliin and allinase which assist in the process.

According to Stoll, alliin is the parent of the germ-fighting process. It's broken down in the body by the enzyme allinase. All it takes is the cutting or crushing of the garlic clove to start the process which produces allicin. And it's this small action that unleashes the healing power of garlic.

Garlic in Your Blood

Legend says that the infamous Count Dracula and his fellow vampires dread only three things: the light of the sun, the sign of the cross and garlic.

That's actually an accurate compliment for garlic, long renowned as the healer of blood that would certainly threaten a blood drainer like Dracula! In fact, there's so much evidence supporting garlic's purgative and cleansing effect on our cardiovascular system, there have been world congresses to study the research.

At the First World Congress on the Health Significance of Garlic and Garlic Constituents in 1990 in Washington, D.C., the chairman, Dr. Robert Lin, said that garlic is an effective tool to lower blood cholesterol and triglyceride levels, reducing blood

BLBBPFFF!

🐝 🐝 🐝 🐝

clots and boosting the immune system. He also stated that garlic's anti-cancer fighting properties have been clearly demonstrated as well as its anti-oxidant or anti-aging properties. This prestigious endorsement is just one of many recent announcements hailing garlic as a wonder food.

In lab studies, garlic has been shown to be effective in reducing the levels of artery-clogging lipids or fats. It also reduces the levels of low-density lipoprotein, or LDL, often called "bad cholesterol."

Dr. Martyn Bailey, of Georgetown University in Washington, D.C., has produced evidence that there's a chemical in garlic called adenosine which blocks the production of the blood compound fribonolytic, which causes clotting.

Dr. Eric Block, of the State University of New York, demonstrated that garlic has the ability to "thin the blood" when adenosine teams with another compound, ajoene.

The awesome twosome are extremely effective anticoagulants, says Block, as effective as aspirin without any of the potentially harmful side effects.

According to a very famous Indian study, three groups of the Jain religious sect further illustrated garlic's powerful blood-cleansing ability. At one extreme were members who feasted on more than a pound of onions and seventeen garlic cloves weekly. These people showed low levels of blood triglycerides and cholesterol levels at the conclusion of test results.

The more orthodox sector of Jains, who had abstained from garlic and onions all their lives, showed just the opposite results. They had elevated triglyceride and cholesterol levels in their blood. The moderate group, which ate moderate amounts of the allium family, fell smack dab in the middle.

Even skeptics are beginning to realize that garlic is a powerful tool for the bloodstream. Until a short while ago, Dr. Marvin Moser, a clinical professor of medicine at Yale University, thought the curative powers of garlic were just another old wives' tale.

"Yeah, and I bet it makes you sexier, too," he once joked at a national conference. "But I looked at over two hundred papers on garlic," he reports, and confirms that many studies did indeed support the fact that garlic lowers blood pressure and has a beneficial effect on the vascular system. "I hope maybe we can start using something natural like garlic instead of drugs."

In 1987, Dr. Benjamin Lau and his colleagues at Loma Linda University in California used Kyolic, the Japanese garlic extract, in a heart disease experiment that had dramatic effects. They found that about a gram of Kyolic (the equivalent of nine cloves of fresh garlic) lowered total cholesterol levels about ten percent on the average and as much as fifty percent in some test subjects! It also lowered the LDL, bad cholesterol, in some people by a whopping seventy percent.

Dr. Hans Reuter of Cologne, West Germany, claimed that garlic is effective for controlling not only cholesterol levels in the blood, but also for lowering blood pressure and removing fatty, dangerous deposits in the arteries. Reuter recommended one to three cloves of raw garlic daily to produce this health-giving benefit.

These are just a few of the many exciting studies linking garlic with improvement of the cardiovascular system. Dr. Paul Saltman, of the University of California in San Diego, says in his experience as a biology professor, he's convinced that garlic does help prevent heart disease by keeping the blood running smoothly.

"Besides the scientific evidence," he says. "There is so much anecdotal evidence to show that eating garlic keeps your blood and heart healthy by preventing clots. Garlic is not only the ounce of prevention in many cardiovascular diseases, it may also be the pound of cure."

———

❧   ❧   ❧   ❧

Garlic Fights Cancer

There's a growing body of scientific research that suggests garlic and its cousins in the allium family reduce the risk of cancer, notably stomach and colon cancers.

This exciting proposal is currently being investigated by none other than the National Institutes of Health, as we mentioned earlier in the introduction. In the next few years, researchers all over the country will try to uncover just how garlic manages to reduce and even kill cancer cells in the body.

Dr. Terrance Leighton, chairman of microbiology and immunology at the University of California at Berkeley, claims the compound in garlic that has anti-carcinogenic effects is called quercetin, which is also present in lesser levels in broccoli, squash and other fruits and vegetables. This theory may in some way explain why people who eat lots of these kinds of foods have a lower incidence of cancer, according to studies.

In addition to American research, Chinese studies reveal that those who eat large quantities of garlic and onions have a twenty-fold lower risk of developing stomach cancer.

Another study showed that rats fed large amounts of quercetin and exposed to carcinogens developed twenty-five percent fewer tumors than the rodents that were not fed quercetin.

At the present time there are more than 1,000 research papers that tout garlic's anti-carcinogenic effects! And since many experts believe that a full thirty-five to sixty percent of all cancers may be caused by dietary factors, using natural foods like garlic is an exciting and most logical approach to tackling this dreaded disease. If we could just look at cancer prevention from a holistic viewpoint, think of the thousands of lives and millions of dollars that might be saved!

One of the most shocking yet encouraging reports on the effect of garlic and cancer was conducted by biologist Michael Wargovich at Houston's Anderson Hospital and Tumor Institute. The doctor gave mice another cancer-fighting compound found in garlic called S allyl-cystene and then exposed them to a chemical known to cause cancer of the colon.

Compared to the control group which did not receive the compound, the garlic-assisted mice developed seventy-five percent fewer tumors. When he repeated the experiment with a chemical that causes cancer in the esophagus, he got even more dramatic results.

"We were stunned and shocked by the end of that experiment," Wargovich says. "Even though the garlic-treated animals were exposed to one of the most potent carcinogens around, not one developed cancer."

In similar studies by George Barany and Lee Wattenberg at the University of Minnesota, and by Sidney Belman at New York University Medical Center, garlic-derived sulfur compounds inhibited tumors of the stomach and the skin.

Garlic also has bioflavonoids, the cancer-fighters in cauliflower and Brussels sprouts, says toxicologist Herbert Pierson, formerly of the National Cancer Institute. The bioflavonoids deliver a double-whammy effect on warding off cancer.

How garlic acts to beat cancer is still a scientific mystery, but some researchers speculate that sulfur molecules are highly active and bind with the metal factors in our blood to prevent the harmful effects of oxygen, which destroys cells.

Although many researchers insist that only fresh garlic works to perform these healing miracles, Dr. Benjamin Lau, a microbiologist at Loma Linda University used the Japanese odorless extract, Kyolic, in his animal experiments. He found that Kyolic was equally effective as fresh garlic in preventing tumors in animals and reducing blood cholesterol in humans.

The odorless supplement, which is available in health food stores across the country, was also tested by a Florida physician, Tarig Abdullah.

Each day, he gave three healthy volunteers six Kyolic capsules, three others one to three bulbs of garlic and a third group of three volunteers no garlic supplementation at all.

He then measured the activity of the blood's natural killer cells, one of the immune system's defenses against the growth of tumors and viruses. After three weeks, he says, the natural killer cells of those who took garlic were "more vicious." They killed twice the number of cancer cells than the control group.

Dr. Abdullah began eating raw garlic cloves daily and hasn't had a cold since 1973!

Garlic as an Antibiotic

Happily, what garlic can do inside your body, it can also do outside. Garlic has been nicknamed nature's antibiotic for good reason. It has saved millions of lives before modern antibiotics arrived on the medical scene and has been touted as a miracle healer of wounds and infections for centuries.

When a garlic clove is crushed, the first compound formed is allicin, which was formally identified in 1944 by Dr. Chester Cavallito as the known antibiotic.

During World War I, British medics wrapped wounds in garlic-soaked bandages to prevent infection, a procedure that saved thousands of wounded soldiers. In the Commonwealth of Independent States, formerly the Soviet Union, garlic is hailed as "Russian penicillin." It was used extensively during World War II to treat Soviet troops.

On one occasion, officials imported five-hundred tons of garlic to combat a flu outbreak. The Russians used garlic as a remedy for colds, whooping cough and intestinal disorders. Polish children are often given garlic preparations for stomach disorders.

In its natural form, allicin, the active antibiotic in garlic, is more potent than penicillin because it attacks twenty-three different kinds of bacteria, including staph and salmonella. It also destroys more than sixty kinds of yeast and fungi infections.

In a current pilot project, researchers are investigating garlic's ability to beat the AIDS virus. Garlic not only helps destroy dangerous viruses and bacteria, it also helps boost the body's immune system which would greatly enhance the fight against deadly AIDS.

❧ ❧ ❧ ❧

Garlic KO's the Flu

Since our family has adopted the garlic-a-day habit, we have been remarkably free from the rounds of flu and other viruses that strike many of our friends and co-workers. Colds just can't catch us!

Many cultures throughout history and in modern society firmly trust in garlic to prevent colds and the flu. In fact, an exciting research project by Dr. James North, chief of microbiology at Brigham Young University in Provo, Utah, showed that garlic is a potent virus killer.

His data proved that garlic extract kills the following viruses with nearly a hundred-percent effectiveness:

- Human rhino virus, which causes colds.
- Parainfluenza 3, a common flu and respiratory virus.
- Herpes simplex 1, which causes fever blisters.
- Herpes simplex 2, which is responsible for genital herpes.

Colorado nutrition counselor Eleonore Blaurock-Busch, president and director of Trace Minerals International, a clinical laboratory in Boulder, has this to say about garlic's effectiveness in soothing sore throats:

"Garlic is one of the best natural antibiotic and antiseptics. Take a 15-grain garlic capsule six times daily and you'll feel better fast."

Dr. Busch is a delightful German-born doctor who says that garlic is one of the best healing foods she has used in her practice.

Dr. Howard Druce, an assistant professor of internal medicine and director of Nasal and Paranasal Sinus Physiology at St. Louis University School of Medicine in Missouri, adds that eating foods rich in spices, especially garlic, helps loosen mucus to relieve stuffy noses.

In other recent studies, garlic killed the polio virus in the lab with ninety-percent effectiveness and made a valiant attempt at tackling the deadly HIV or AIDS-producing virus. This discovery has prompted quite a few scientists to look into the possibility of a natural AIDS cure based on garlic's amazing healing powers not only as an immune booster, but as a destroyer of the actual killer cells.

In fact, the minerals selenium and germanium, found in abundance in garlic, are prime targets for AIDS research. Researchers have learned these powerful compounds are terrific in battling many elusive viruses and body cancers.

Garlic Fights Breast Cancer

There is exciting new research that indicates how effective garlic can be in fighting breast cancer. Dr. Robert Lin, the executive vice president for Nutrition International, says he is encouraged by the reports from Sloan Kettering Cancer Center in New York.

Researchers at Sloan Kettering found that garlic extract stopped the growth in breast cancer cells by more than fifty percent. Their evidence suggests eating two to three medium cloves of garlic daily or the equivalent can potentially reduce the risk of breast cancer, as well as other cancers, by ten to one-hundred percent.

Dr. Lin, who has been investigating the healing powers of garlic for some time, recommends putting fresh garlic into soups, roasts and stir-fries. He doesn't suggest relying on garlic powders for a healing effect. He does advocate the use of Kyolic, which is readily available in health food stores.

"Combining all the evidence," says Lin, "it's beyond any doubt that adequate garlic consumption can help fight cancers—including breast cancer." Dr. Lin, along with Dr. John Pinto of Sloan Kettering and Dr. Fillmore Freeman of the University of California at Irvine, discovered that aged garlic extract effectively inhibits the growth of cancer cells cultured in test tubes during a recent project at the University of Arizona.

It's important to note, however, that experts also recommend eating a low-fat diet—under thirty percent of calories coming from fat—to further reduce the risk of dangerous breast cancer. It's unfortunate, but most American women consume about forty-percent fat in their daily diet.

૨ઢ   ૨ઢ   ૨ઢ   ૨ઢ

More Garlic Cures

In the scope of this book, there is only room for the tip of the iceberg when it comes to research projects that have shown how effective garlic is in healing the body. There are many more possibilities.

For example, there is evidence that garlic nourishes the brain and is a great intelligence booster. The U. S. Department of Agriculture's Human Nutrition Center in Beltsville, Maryland demonstrated that the herb not only lowers the levels of blood fat, but also blood sugar.

This makes garlic a form of diabetes control. In fact, Dr. Ronald Hoffman advises his patients who have diabetes to supplement their diet with garlic, along with other vitamins and minerals.

"Diabetics tend to develop yeast infections more because yeast thrives in a high-sugar environment," Dr. Hoffman says. "Garlic suppresses yeast. The deodorized capsules are best."

The late Dr. Paavo Airola, who once said he ate everything but fruit with garlic, claimed the clove can treat the following list of ailments:

- high blood pressure
- arteriosclerosis
- tuberculosis
- diabetes
- cancer
- hypoglycemia
- bronchitis
- asthma
- whooping cough
- pneumonia
- the common cold
- allergies
- intestinal worms
- intestinal disorders and gas
- parasitic diarrhea
- dysentery
- insomnia.

Dr. Airola said he treated his patients with garlic for all of the above conditions and commented:

"One of the most effective ways to arrest an approaching sore throat type of cold is to cut a clove of garlic in half and keep both halves in the mouth for several hours, if possible."

Whew! I hope Mrs. Airola liked garlic breath!

Garlic has important anti-aging minerals, selenium and germanium, adding another dimension to its royal reputation.

"I think garlic is an extremely important healing and anti-aging food," says Dr. Ronald Klatz, of the American Longevity Institute in Chicago. "Garlic is one of the most perfect anti-aging and disease fighting foods we have. I wish more medical experts would prescribe garlic to their patients to preserve the cardiovascular system, prevent disease and, of course, retard the aging process."

Even Dr. William Castelli, the director of the world's most famous study on heart disease and cholesterol (the Framingham study in Massachusetts), includes garlic on his list of foods that contribute to the prevention of heart disease.

In light of all this research, why hasn't the world heard more about this wonderful, powerful but natural drug? I think it's best summed up in this statement by Ross S. Feldberg, associate professor of biology at Tufts University.

"So why has the U.S. medical establishment shown such a low level of interest in the medicinal uses of garlic? The answer is probably an economic one...The costs of establishing the efficiency and safety of any new pharmaceutical are quite high. Yet, there is little profit to be made in marketing a folk remedy that people can obtain quite cheaply and administer to themselves."

Garlic and Fleas

I used to think the addition of garlic to an animal's food to ward off fleas was simply an old wives' tale. But this method of flea-control has been extremely effective for our four pets.

Indeed, Dr. Richard Pitcairn, a noted holistic veterinarian, recommends serving garlic to your pet daily to repel fleas. He says it helps boost an animals' immune system, eliminates worms, aids in digestion and stimulates the intestinal tract.

Garlic helps regulate your pet's weight, too, and should be given to overweight and lethargic dogs to add years of healthful vigor to their lives. Dr. Pitcairn says he's had success treating animals with arthritis and hip dysplasia using garlic, and recommends from a half clove to three cloves per day, depending on the dog's size.

Andi Brown, an entrepreneur from Tampa, makes the best pure and natural animal products around, and uses an abundance of garlic oil in her wonderful skin-care product, called Dream Coat.

"Garlic oil is a natural antibiotic and helps boost the animal's immune system," she explains. "It stimulates the animal's digestive tract and is a great blood purifier. When the blood is pure, fleas aren't attracted. Since the skin is also soft and supple, the fleas have nothing to burrow into.

"Often people think it's the smell of garlic that repels the fleas, but I believe when the animal is healthy, fleas just are not attracted."

Andi also uses lots of garlic (almost a whole head as well as two whole onions) in her homemade pet food, which includes chicken, brown rice and vegetables. We include one of her recipes in the last chapter of the book for those interested in preserving their pets' health as well as their own!

Noted retired veterinarian Gloria Dodd, of Gualala, California, has been using garlic, particularly the Kyolic liquid, to help treat sick animals for years.

"I also use Kyolic liquid to preserve the good health of my clients' pets," says Dr. Dodd. "In my practice, I have found that garlic successfully eliminates toxins and other poisonous substances from their organs.

"In our valley, we had a bothersome outbreak of toxemia a few years back due to a parvo epidemic. The percentage of dogs that were dying from toxemia was very high when they were treated with orthodox methods. However, when we added Kyolic to their medicine, I had a much higher success rate of treatment."

Dodd advises using liquid garlic supplements for both dogs and cats to keep their organs healthy and to maintain normal digestion, no matter what the cause of upset.

She gives small dogs about one-half teaspoon three times a day and increases the dosage up to one tablespoon, three times a day for larger breeds.

"I firmly believe that Kyolic strengthens the immune system and helps repel parasites," Dr. Dodd says. "I've spoken to many other veterinarians who have used garlic to alleviate the symptoms of high fever, diarrhea, coughing and other diseases. Even horses benefit from liquid garlic in their diet."

Many breeders use garlic to keep their pets' coats shiny and healthy. One of my yellow Labradors developed a nasty fungal infection last summer. He had red sores all over his body and patches of fur were falling off.

I took my own advice and used liquid garlic in his food. Sure enough, in less than two weeks, his coat was back to its lustrous condition and all the red spots had disappeared.

"In my opinion, every disease is an accumulation of toxins," says Dr. Dodd. "It doesn't matter if the illness is chemical, viral or bacterial in nature. Therefore, since garlic is a natural detoxifier, it's the best prevention against disease. I confess that I, along with all my own cats and dogs, take it daily."

This hefty endorsement for garlic is repeated by one of America's most beloved actresses, June Lockhart, who many of us remember fondly as Lassie's human mother in the TV series.

Lockhart's pet dog, Tony, developed a severe flea problem. Someone suggested she add garlic to the dog's food and when she did, she was pleased to discover that it worked.

"Now I keep several bottles of liquid garlic—I can't stand the smell of fresh on hand," she says. "I'm truly a garlic convert."

Garlic can be used externally, too, to treat pets. A friend of mine noticed that her dog, Nikki, had developed a limp. The pup's toe was red and swollen, so she took her to a reputable clinic.

"The doctors told me nothing was wrong and that Nikki would heal by herself," she says. "But the problem grew steadily worse and Nikki was in agony. I took her back and the vet made an incision. They found a small lump but said this was not the problem. They closed the incision and applied antibiotic creams and bandages."

Nikki's foot did not get better and my friend was told the toe may have to be amputated. In desperation, she applied Kyolic to the affected area.

"I had heard so much about the healing power of garlic that I decided to give it a shot," my friend recalls. "I soaked her wound with a cotton ball dipped in liquid garlic repeatedly and left some on the wound. I covered it with a bandage. I also fed her liquid garlic. She actually loved the taste!"

By the end of the second day of the garlic treatment, the swelling was going down and the incision had begun to close. By the end of the third day, the incision was completely closed and the toe, although it was still red, was almost its normal size.

My friend was elated. She took Nikki back to the clinic to show the vets.

"They were amazed," she says. "They told me to continue the liquid garlic treatment."

By the way, liquid garlic has also been found to be effective in treating human fungal infections and wounds. Try some under your nails if you develop a fungus. A little liquid garlic on a Q-tip or toothpick can help solve even the most hard-to-treat areas.

Garlic Fights Allergies

There is also a mounting body of evidence that by boosting the body's immune system, garlic can help reduce your allergic response to many environmental toxins.

"I get hundreds of letters from happy folks who have had remarkable results from simply adding garlic to their diet," says Charlie Fox, of Wakunaga of America Co., Ltd., the company that manufactures Kyolic.

"We get testimonials from people who solved severe stomach problems like ulcers, diabetes, depression, even undetermined illnesses," Fox says. "I remember the happy mom who wrote to me about her son, Judson, who was only six years old, but had been suffering from numerous allergy-related symptoms for years. His tonsils hurt, he had ear aches, he wouldn't eat—you name it and he had it.

"She had taken him to a variety of specialists who dispensed medication and told her he'd have to have his tonsils out. One day, she got so sick and tired of giving Jud antibiotics she switched to garlic capsules, three times a day. She wrote to us that not only his physical and medical condition improved, his behavior has been a lot better."

Interestingly, one of the most unusual testimonials came from Dr. Ritchi Morris of Ardsley, New York. As a sports psychologist and naturopath, Morris has been using garlic supplementation successfully for years to help professional athletes. He's helped many players from New York's Giants, Rangers, Knicks and Yankees, as well as world-class Olympic athletes, improve their performance and stamina.

"I found that when I added Kyolic to their diet, they played better and had fewer bouts with depression," writes Morris. "It's been particularly effective for weight lifters and runners because garlic helps break down fat and prevent the buildup of lactic acids in the cooled down muscles."

Morris further believes that garlic, because of its immune-boosting properties, helps reduce the stress of competition in professional athletes.

Garlic as an Insecticide

According to Lloyd Harris in *The Book of Garlic,* this herb has long been an effective and environmentally safe insecticide. It kills a variety of plant destroying bugs and larvae without poisoning the air around us.

Harris recommends planting garlic in your garden to help ward off insects as well as harvesting your own allium delights. Many organic gardeners border their plantings with rows of garlic just for this reason.

They also spray their plants with a garlic-based solution. Here's one developed by British researcher David Greenstock that Harris claims is highly effective:

"Take three ounces of chopped garlic and let it soak in two teaspoons of mineral oil for twenty-four hours. Then slowly add a pint of water in which one-quarter ounce of oil-base soap, like Palmolive, has been dissolved. Stir well.

"Strain liquid through fine gauze and store in a china or glass container to prevent a reaction to metals. Use it in a dilution of one part to twenty of water to begin with, then one to one hundred thereafter. Apply to plants as a spray."

As more of us turn to organic gardening for health and survival, we might do well to take note of this helpful formula and preserve not only the fruits of our labor, but also our environment and our good health.

As we all know, chemical sprays have come under scrutiny over the past decades and many people are already suffering from allergic reactions to the pollutants in our air and food. The further we stray from nature, the more our bodies will rebel.

That's why garlic is such a wonder food. Its uses are so varied and its health-giving benefits so bountiful, there are almost limitless horizons in garlic's future. The sooner you begin putting garlic in your daily diet, on your plants and into your life, the healthier you'll be.

Ode to Garlic

There's one city in the United States that thrives on garlic in many ways. Gilroy, California is hailed as the "Garlic Capital of the World." It boasts a $54-million-a-year garlic industry in a town with only a 27,400 population.

Gilroy is located eighty miles south of San Francisco in the fertile Santa Clara Valley and houses two of the major dehydration plants and three of the major fresh garlic shippers in the world.

Humorist Will Rogers once joked that Gilroy is "the only town in America where you can marinate a steak by hanging it on the clothesline," referring to the pungent odor that permeates the city.

The residents of Gilroy are used to jibes and jokes, but they're laughing all the way to the bank. A full ninety percent of the garlic con-

sumed in fifty states is shipped through Gilroy for processing and packaging, much of it grown within a ninety-mile radius of the city.

The Gilroy-based Fresh Garlic Association reports Americans gobble twenty-four ounces of whole garlic per person each year. That's about twenty bulbs per capita or five billion heads a year!

Each year, the folks in Gilroy hold their famous annual garlic festival on the last weekend of July. This gigantic event began in 1979 and has attracted millions of curious visitors who want to learn more about the storage and preparation of garlic—as well as try new and innovative ways to use the bulb in recipes.

Festival goers also have a chance to participate in Garlic Golf, Love That Garlic Tennis Tournament, Miss Garlic Contest and the Tour de Garlique Country Bicycle Tour.

(For more information on the Gilroy Festival, write to P. O. Box 2311, Gilroy, California 95020.)

Another famous garlic gathering occurs in Berkeley, California. It's sponsored by the Lovers of the Stinking Rose society and is held in mid-July each year. The Berkeley Garlic Festival features more than 50 restaurants that create garlic-only menus for the event for a two-week period. (Contact Lovers of the Stinking Rose, 1621 Fifth Street, Berkeley, California 94710 for more information.)

The annual Garlic Fest in Covington, Kentucky, is held every February and features cook-offs, a bulb-peeling contest and Miss Garlic beauty pageant. (For more information, write to Coving Haus, 100 West Sixth Street, Covington, Kentucky 41011.)

And in Massachusetts, there's the annual Fitchburg Garlic Festival that's held every June in a most appropriate location, an Italian church!

Garlic in America

Most of the garlic on our shelves comes from California, where ninety percent of the crops are grown. The quality of American garlic is considered to be superior and the range, incredible. Different kinds of garlic are grown in various counties, ranging in color from white to dark wine.

Garlic bulbs can grow as many as twelve cloves or as few as four. Some varieties have stubby cloves while others are long and narrow.

Commercial growers value the Late, Early, Chileno, Chilean and Egyptian strains for their dependability and hardiness. Most of the garlic consumed in the United States comes from five California counties: Monterey, San Benito and Santa Clara on the coast, and from Fresno and Kern in the interior valleys. Over 250 million pounds of garlic are produced each year in plantings on more than 21,000 acres.

The majority of garlic grown in California is dehydrated and used in manufacturing ketchup, mustard, sausage and pickles. It also appears in salts and powders commonly found on household shelves for easy flavoring. Some of the garlic produced becomes garlic powder pills and oils available in health food stores.

Odorless pills and liquids, such as Kyolic, are extremely popular for health-giving and socially acceptable benefits. For those who fear garlic breath or don't like the odor altogether, this may be the way to get garlic's health benefits in a more palatable form.

The most common types of commercially grown garlic are:

- Late garlic, a variety that keeps very well. It's characterized by narrow, upright dark green leaves and a white sheath surrounding the clove. The clove itself ranges in color from light pink to deep red.

- Early garlic, as the name implies, harvests earlier than the previous variety. It has broader leaves and appears pale green in color. You'll also note purplish veins in the skin.
- Creole garlic, commonly grown in Mexico and South America. This plant resembles Late garlic but is taller and lighter in color. The skin covering the cloves is dark pink.
- Chileno garlic is a variation of the Creole but with larger, more robust cloves.
- Egyptian garlic, a tall and fast-growing variety. This popular gourmet garlic produces large white bulbs that contain many small cloves in white sheaths.
- Elephant garlic is quite popular in culinary circles because of its mild flavor. The large bulb is almost the size of a tennis ball.
- Italian garlic, commonly grown in Louisiana and other sub-tropical parts of this country. Its pink or purplish cloves are stronger in flavor and smaller than the Creole, which is also grown in Louisiana.
- Silverskin garlic is perhaps the most commonly used in the country. This variety is characterized by the familiar white outer covering of the bulbs. It's also the best bet for novice growers because it's so hardy.
- Spanish Rojo, or Spanish Red, garlic is powerfully flavored and originated in Spain.
- Rocombole is also called the "serpent garlic" because of its coiled, looping shape. The bulbs are smaller in size than conventionally shaped garlic, but its flavor is just as pungent. The baby bulbs can be eaten fresh and are delicious in salads.

Growing and Harvesting Your Own Garlic

Experts say that growing your own garlic is surprisingly easy. Garlic does not produce true seeds, but must be propagated by individual cloves planted at a uniform depth for consistent germination.

It's important to keep the plants thoroughly watered to a depth of two feet until they reach full growth and the tops begin to show signs of yellowing. That's when irrigation stops and garlic fields are allowed to dry out for harvest.

Garlic plants are harvested when ninety percent of the tops are brown and dry. Usually, harvesting begins in June and continues through September. Once gathered, the bulbs are covered with leaves and straw, and placed in the wind's path to dry.

Since the flavor of garlic comes from carefully curing, this process is extremely important to the grower. The curing time depends on the size of the plants, and, of course, the weather. When the sheath covering the bulb is dry and paper-like in texture and the root crown is hard, the garlic is ready for general consumption.

After three weeks of ideal curing, commercially grown garlic is then trimmed by hand, graded and sorted. Most of the garlic is placed in cardboard cartons for shipment to market. In the supermarket, you'll find garlic sold in bulk or in packages containing two or three bulbs.

If you're curing garlic at home, choose a cool, dry spot. Basements or garages are fine. Once cured, you can braid the stems to form attractive bunches or store them in mesh bags. Old nylon stockings or wire racks are also ideal storage vehicles for garlic bulbs.

ᕤ   ᕤ   ᕤ   ᕤ

When you buy garlic, look for firm plump bulbs with clean, dry, unbroken skin. Once you bring it home, store garlic in a cool, dry place in an open container. Experts don't advise storing garlic in the refrigerator because of the dampness.

You can also chop or puree garlic cloves and store them in jars. To preserve the flavor, mix a little olive oil or lemon juice with the end product. Let the puree ripen for at least a day before using it in your favorite recipes. By the way, garlic is a dieter's delight, so feel free to spice up your favorite dishes. Each clove contains a few calories, depending on the size.

Dehydrate garlic by slicing the cloves into thin slices and laying them on cheesecloth to dry either in the sun or in a gas oven with the pilot light on. Once the slices become brittle chips, store them in a tightly sealed jar in a cool cupboard. Once again, refrigeration is not recommended because of the dampness which can spoil stored garlic.

It's easy to create custom-designed, marinated garlic by covering sliced cloves with the best olive oil you can afford, and including freshly snipped herbs and spices.

To peel a clove, hit it with the flat side of a large knife blade (like a cleaver) and then cut across the root end, peeling the skin upward. Twenty seconds in the microwave will also loosen the husks and make peeling easier. Large amounts of garlic can be dropped in boiling water for a few minutes, then plunged into cold water to cool down. The peel then slips off easily.

For maximum flavor, handle garlic carefully. Long, slow cooking makes the flavor and potency more delicate. Garlic is most robust and powerful eaten raw, either minced or pressed straight from the clove. A garlic press is a great kitchen tool that helps you extract maximum flavor from the succulent clove, but many chefs rely on the side of a knife to extract garlic's flavor.

When you are sautéing garlic in a pan for a particular recipe, don't scorch or burn it. This gives garlic a bitter flavor. Use medium to medium-low heat and gently sauté the cloves or garlic preparations for about three minutes. Cook just until the herb becomes translucent.

To ease garlic breath, eat fresh parsley or rinse your mouth with lemon juice. You can also try chewing on a coffee or vanilla bean (or, better still, hang around with fellow garlic lovers so that you won't notice the odor). Ordinary mouthwash doesn't work because the odor of garlic oozes through your body's pores, say experts. You'd have to bathe in mouthwash to eliminate the odor!

Remember that the longer you store garlic in the open air, the milder it becomes. If your bulb develops sprouts after prolonged storage, don't fret. This doesn't mean the bulb has gone bad.

Store garlic powders and other dehydrated forms away from the stove and windows with direct sunlight streaming in. Heat and light can reduce the natural flavor from processed garlic.

In Italy, chefs prepare a sumptuous garlic bread called "bruschetta" simply by rubbing garlic cloves on the crusty perimeter of sliced, toasted bread and topping the slices with chopped tomatoes, mushrooms and olive oil.

You can also bake garlic by removing the outer layers of skin, drizzling each clove with olive oil and sprinkling with oregano. Wrap the garlic in foil and bake at 375 degrees for an hour. The nutty, sweet cloves make an excellent and unusual appetizer—terrific with roast meats, fowl or fish.

Sources for Garlic Lovers

There are plenty of books and literature on the market praising both the healing powers and the use of garlic. Here are some additional sources of information:

The Unknown Miracle Worker by Yoshio Kato
This book was originally printed in Japan but is currently available through Japan Publications Trading Company, 1174 Howard Street, San Francisco, CA 94100

The Miracle Of Garlic by Paavo Airola
Health Plus, P. O. Box 22001, Phoenix, Arizona 85028

The Book Of Garlic by Lloyd John Harris
Aris Books, 1621 Fifth Street, Berkeley, CA 94710

The Official Garlic Lovers Handbook by Lloyd John Harris
Also published by Aris Books

The Complete Garlic Lover's Cookbook: From Gilroy, Garlic Capital of the World, Celestial Arts Press, P. O. Box 7327, Berkeley, CA 94707

"The Chemistry Of Garlic And Onions"
Scientific American, March 1985, Volume 252, No. 3

Healing AIDS Naturally by Laurence Badgely, M.D.
Human Energy Press, 370 West Bruno Avenue,
Suite D, San Bruno, CA 94066

The Food Pharmacy by Jean Carper
Bantam, 66 Fifth Avenue, New York, NY 10103

Fresh Garlic Association
Attn: Caryl Saunders Associates, P. O. Box 2410, Sausalito, CA
94966-2410

Recipes

MUSHROOM BUTTONS

4 servings

Simple fare with a remarkable flavor—thanks to garlic!

1 pound large mushrooms	2 cloves garlic, minced
¼ cup chopped onion	1 teaspoon grated Parmesan cheese

Preheat broiler.

Wash mushrooms well and pat dry. Remove stems and chop fine. Sauté stems with onion and garlic in a non-stick frying pan over medium heat for 5 minutes. Fill caps with this mixture. Sprinkle with Parmesan cheese. Place mushrooms in a broiler-proof casserole or pie plate. Broil for 5 minutes. Serve warm.

NOTE: You may also add ½ cup chopped, fresh spinach to the stuffing mixture.

MICROWAVE VEGETABLE PLATTER

6 servings

So easy to prepare, but it looks like a dish fit for a king!

1 cup broccoli flowerets
1 cup cauliflower
1 cup carrot sticks
2 zucchini squash,
    cut into julienne sticks

1 each red and green peppers,
    cut into strips
1 tablespoon lemon juice
2 tablespoons minced garlic
Salt and freshly ground pepper,
    to taste

Arrange the broccoli, cauliflower and carrot sticks around the outer edge of a microwave-safe pie plate or dish. Place the rest of the vegetables neatly in the center, in separate piles. Sprinkle with garlic and lemon juice. Cover with plastic wrap and microwave on high for 5 minutes. Let stand 5 minutes before serving.

ANTIPASTO SALAD

2 servings

This appetizer or light luncheon is great for the single student or solitary diner who wants taste and nutrition with little fuss and effort.

1 6-ounce can water-
    packed tuna, drained
1 teaspoon minced garlic
2 cups fresh broccoli

2 cups cauliflower,
4 carrots cut into $\frac{1}{4}$ inch slices
2 cups romaine lettuce
$\frac{1}{4}$ cup fat-free Italian salad
    dressing

Steam vegetables until tender-crisp. Mix the tuna, garlic and vegetables with the dressing until well blended. Chill at least 30 minutes. Serve atop the romaine. This mixture is also good spooned into a pita bread for lunch.

BAKED STUFFED TOMATO

4 servings

You can double, triple or otherwise multiply this recipe.

4 medium tomatoes
1 cup chopped broccoli,
   steamed or microwaved
   until crisp
1 teaspoon minced garlic

2 tablespoons soft bread crumbs
1 teaspoon oregano
2 tablespoons grated Parmesan
   cheese
Salt and freshly ground pepper, to
   taste

Preheat oven to 400°.

Cut tomatoes in half and scoop out pulp. Combine pulp, broccoli, garlic, salt, pepper, bread crumbs and oregano. Stuff each tomato half with broccoli mixture and sprinkle with Parmesan cheese. Bake for 5 minutes or until bubbly.

EGGPLANT PROVENÇALE

8 servings

Here's a side dish or appetizer that's sure to please.

5 medium eggplants,
   peeled and chopped
Salt and pepper to taste
1 cup olive oil
6 ripe tomatoes, chopped
   and seeds removed
7 cloves garlic, finely chopped

1 tablespoon thyme
1/4 cup seasoned Italian
   bread crumbs
4 anchovy fillets
1 tablespoon flour
1/4 cup milk

Preheat oven to 350°.

Sprinkle the eggplant with a little salt and pepper. In a large skillet, heat 1/2 cup olive oil and sauté the eggplant, tomatoes, garlic and thyme.

Stir in the bread crumbs. Continue cooking over medium-low heat while mashing the vegetables with a fork until they are tender.

In a small skillet, heat the remaining oil with the anchovies. Add the flour and mix well. Stir in the milk. Stir the anchovy mixture into the eggplant mixture and transfer the whole mixture into a two-quart buttered casserole dish. Bake 30 minutes or until golden. Serve hot.

❧ ❧ ❧ ❧

Spicy Artichoke Hearts

6 servings

This unusual dish is the ideal first course for any dinner party.

2 10-ounce cans quartered artichoke hearts, rinsed and squeezed dry

2 cups salt-free salsa

1 clove garlic, minced

$\frac{1}{2}$ cup tomato sauce

1 teaspoon oregano or Italian herb blend

A few drops hot pepper sauce

1 tablespoon fresh parsley, for garnish

Combine all the ingredients except parsley in a bowl. Stir to blend. Sprinkle with parsley and chill at least one hour in the refrigerator before serving. Serve with hot bread or tortilla chips.

Curry Dip

Makes 1 $\frac{1}{2}$ cups

Here's another exotic dip that has great flavor, thanks to the subtle addition of garlic.

1 cup low-fat cottage cheese

$\frac{1}{2}$ cup fresh parsley

1 scallion, chopped

3 cloves garlic, minced

1 small tomato, chopped

1 teaspoon curry powder (or more if you like spicy food)

Combine all ingredients in a blender and process until smooth. Chill well before serving.

Sweet Potato Chips

These yummy snacks are healthy yet flavorful. You'll never want a commercially prepared potato chip again!

2 pounds yams or sweet potatoes scrubbed and sliced $\frac{1}{8}$-inch thick

2 tablespoons safflower oil

2 tablespoons spicy vegetable, seasoning, like Spike or Mrs. Dash

1 tablespoon garlic salt

Preheat oven to 450°.

Place sliced potatoes in a bowl, sprinkle with oil and mix thoroughly. Spread the potatoes in a single layer on a non-stick baking sheet and sprinkle with vegetable seasoning and garlic salt. Bake for 12 to 15 minutes or until nicely browned. Serve immediately.

NOTE: Baking potatoes can also be used to make oven fries that are simply delicious. I sometimes dip the raw slices in low-calorie Italian dressing instead of oil before baking and sprinkle a little paprika on top for extra zip.

ROASTED GARLIC BEAN DIP

Makes 2 cups

An excellent appetizer dip that's great with pita bread.

10 cloves roasted garlic (see note)	1 tablespoon cider vinegar
	$\frac{1}{2}$ teaspoon ground cumin
1 15-ounce can cannellini drained	$\frac{1}{2}$ cup low-fat yogurt
	2 tablespoon chopped parsley

In a food processor, combine garlic, beans, vinegar and cumin. Process 1 minute, scraping bowl once. Add yogurt and parsley; process until just blended.

Serve with crackers or warm pita bread cut into sections and warmed in the oven.

NOTE: To make roasted garlic, coat unpeeled cloves with olive oil. Bake at 375° for 15 minutes. Cool and peel.

SPINACH DIP

Makes 2 1/2 cups

I have a particular fondness for this easy-to-prepare dip that is very low in fat and offers superb taste. Use as a dip for fresh vegetables or spread on crisp crackers.

1 10-ounce package frozen chopped spinach, thawed drained very well
1/4 cup chopped onion

1 cup low-fat cottage cheese
2 garlic cloves, minced
1 teaspoon Worcestershire sauce
White pepper, to taste

Sauté onion in non-stick pan over medium heat until golden, about 5 minutes. Blend remaining ingredients with onion in a small serving bowl. Chill for at least 30 minutes before serving.

BLUE CHEESE BITES

6 servings

You can double or triple the recipe to serve a crowd!

1 10-ounce package buttermilk biscuits from the dairy case
1/2 cup crumbled blue cheese
1/4 cup melted margarine
1 teaspoon minced garlic

Preheat oven to 400°.

Separate buttermilk biscuits and cut into quarters. Place on a non-stick cookie sheet, 1 inch apart. Sprinkle with blue cheese, melted margarine and garlic. Bake for 15 minutes or until golden brown.

CURRIED YOGURT DIP

Makes 1 cup

This excellent dip tastes like it's made with sour cream but doesn't have the fat and calories of the real thing. It's great for chicken wings, raw vegetables—anything that needs a dip with a real bite!

$^2/_3$ cup plain low-fat yogurt
$^1/_3$ cup sour cream
1 teaspoon curry powder

1 tablespoon minced garlic
1 teaspoon lemon juice
$^1/_4$ teaspoon white pepper

In a bowl, combine all the ingredients, stirring them well. Chill the dip, covered, for 1 hour or longer before serving.

Variation: Omit curry and replace with $^1/_4$ cup chopped, fresh dill.

MOCK CRAB DIP

Makes 1 $^1/_2$ cups

M-M-good! And it doesn't hurt your pocketbook either!

8 ounces low-fat cottage cheese
1 tablespoon minced onion or scallions
1 teaspoon lemon juice

4 ounces imitation crab (surimi)
1 teaspoon Worcestershire sauce
1 tablespoon minced garlic

Shred crab meat with a fork. Combine all ingredients and chill, covered. Serve with whole wheat crackers and/or raw vegetable sticks.

QUICHE

6 servings

This basic quiche recipe can be altered to suit your purposes. Feel free to experiment with different fillings.

1 unbaked 9-inch pie shell	1 cup low-fat yogurt
1 tablespoon butter	$^1/_2$ cup low-fat milk
2 large scallions, sliced	$^1/_2$ teaspoon paprika
2 cloves garlic, chopped	1 cup shredded low-fat cheese
4 slices bacon, chopped	Salt and freshly ground pepper,
3 eggs	to taste

Preheat oven to 400°.

In a large frying pan, heat butter until melted. Stir in scallions, garlic and bacon. Stir and cook over medium heat for 5 minutes or until bacon is crisp. Meanwhile, in a blender, mix eggs, yogurt, milk and salt until smooth. Place the bacon mixture in the pie shell. Pour the yogurt mixture over the bacon. Sprinkle the cheese and spices over the top and bake for about 40 minutes or until set.

VARIATION #1: Add chopped spinach, seafood or just about any leftover vegetable (sliced zucchini is superb!) to the pie shell before adding the yogurt-milk mixture. I love adding 1 package of defrosted and drained frozen spinach and 1 cup of surimi or crab meat.

VARIATION #2: Eliminate the scallions and add 2 cups chopped onion for a very tasty quiche.

CHICKEN LIVER PÂTÉ

Makes 3 cups

Garlic in Mama's chicken liver! Why not? It adds a very special flavor to this traditional recipe.

1 pound chicken livers	$^1/_2$ cup fresh parsley, minced
2 cups water	2 cloves garlic, minced
1 onion, quartered	2 tablespoons brandy
2 hard boiled eggs	Salt and freshly ground pepper, to taste

Boil chicken livers for 10 minutes in water. Add more water if necessary to keep from sticking. Cover and let stand 10 minutes. Process the livers with the remaining ingredients in a blender or food processor, adding a little water from the cooking liquid to make a fine paste.

NOTE: To save time, cook the eggs with the livers. They will be hard cooked after the standing time. For extra flavor, you can also sauté the livers in butter or chicken fat instead of boiling. Add the livers and the butter drippings to the blender or food processor.

Spicy Meatballs

6 servings

Appetizers that are quick to prepare yet taste great.

1 pound lean ground round or turkey	$\frac{1}{2}$ cup flour or bread crumbs
1 1-ounce packet onion soup mix	1 teaspoon minced garlic
$\frac{1}{2}$ cup ketchup or chili sauce	1 teaspoon dried oregano
	Salt and freshly ground pepper, to taste

Mix all ingredients together and form into 1-inch balls. Place in a microwave dish. Cover with vented plastic wrap and microwave on high for 10 minutes, turning the dish twice during cooking. Drain off excess fat and liquid. Serve meatballs with toothpicks.

NOTE: You can also sauté these in a 12-inch skillet. Brown the meatballs over high heat, then simmer for 15 minutes. A little water added to the pan will prevent sticking.

Baked Garlic

8 servings

8 whole heads fresh garlic	4 sprigs fresh rosemary or
2 to 4 tablespoons olive oil	oregano, or 2 teaspoons dried

Remove outer layers of skin from garlic, leaving cloves and head intact. Place all heads on double thickness of foil; top with olive oil and herbs. Fold up and seal. Bake for 1 hour. Serve one whole head per person. Squeeze cooked cloves from skin onto cooked meats or vegetables or on toasted French bread.

VARIATION: You may trim tops off heads to expose tops of garlic cloves. This makes cloves easier to scoop out. Then, bake as instructed. Cooking time will be slightly reduced.

Mushroom and Garlic in Puff Pastry

4 servings

This elegant dish is extremely easy to prepare and a delight to serve.

2 tablespoons olive oil
4 garlic cloves, minced
1 medium onion, diced
1 medium tomato, chopped
1 pound mushrooms,
  cleaned and sliced

2 large eggs, beaten
$\frac{1}{4}$ cup cream
$\frac{1}{2}$ pound store bought
  puff pastry

Preheat the oven to 400°.

Heat oil in a large skillet over medium heat and add the garlic, onion and tomato. Simmer for 10 minutes.

Add the mushrooms and cook, uncovered, 7 minutes more. Remove from heat and cool. Stir in the egg and cream.

Spread or roll the thawed puff pastry into an 11-x-4-inch rectangle, line a shallow lasagna or jelly roll pan and bake for 10 minutes or until lightly puffed. Prick the pastry gently with a fork to deflate it. Add the mushroom mixture and bake for 25 minutes. Let cool for 5 minutes before slicing.

Garlic lends a special appeal to soups, giving them an unequaled richness of flavor. Here's a sampling of both hot and cold soups that owe their tastiness to garlic.

Spanish Garlic Soup

4 servings

This light first-course soup wins top honors for flavor and health-giving properties. You can also use it as a stock to make other dishes such as rice, beans or pasta.

12 cloves garlic, peeled
and chopped
1 teaspoon salt
1 teaspoon white pepper
$\frac{1}{4}$ teaspoon each oregano,
thyme and basil
1 bay leaf

5 cups water or chicken stock
2 tablespoons oil
2 slices whole grain bread,
toasted
Grated Parmesan cheese, to
taste (optional)

Combine garlic, seasonings, water or stock, and oil and bring to a boil in a 5-quart saucepan. Cover and simmer for 30 minutes. Crumble bread into the soup and return to a boil. Serve as is, or topped with grated cheese.

French Garlic Soup

16 servings

The French region of Provence boasts liberal use of garlic in its cuisine. This great soup has lots of aromatic garlic!

2 tablespoons olive oil
1 cup chopped garlic
¼ cup chopped shallots
2 medium carrots,
　chopped fine
½ cup flour

1 cup dry red wine
1 gallon chicken stock
2 bay leaves
2 tablespoons minced parsley
1 ½ cups lentils
Salt and freshly ground pepper,
　to taste

In a large stock pot, heat the olive oil over medium heat and sauté the garlic, shallots and carrots until tender. Add flour and mix well. Add the wine and stir until smooth. Add the stock, bay leaves, parsley and lentils.

Bring the mixture to a boil and simmer until lentils are tender (about 25 minutes). Season with salt and pepper.

Greek Lentil Soup

8 servings

Being of Greek descent, I am particularly fond of this soup.

2 tablespoons olive oil
2 medium onions, chopped
2 stalks celery, chopped
2 carrots, chopped
8 cups water
1 6-ounce can tomato paste

2 cloves garlic, chopped
1 bay leaf
2 cups dried lentils
4 cups shredded spinach
Salt and white pepper, to taste
3 tablespoons lemon juice

Heat oil in a large saucepan and sauté onion until soft. Add remaining ingredients except spinach and lemon juice. Mix well. Bring to a boil, cover and simmer 1 hour. Add spinach and seasonings to taste and cook 10 minutes more. Stir in lemon juice and serve.

🐜　🐜　🐜　🐜

EASY VEGETABLE SOUP

4 servings

This quick healthful soup tastes like it was simmered for hours.

2 medium carrots, cut into
   1/2 -inch slices
2 stalks celery, cut into
   1-inch slices
1/2 cup onion
3 cloves garlic, chopped

2 cups water, divided
2 cups tomato juice
1 teaspoon soy sauce
1 teaspoon oregano
1 tablespoon butter or olive oil
Salt and pepper, to taste

Place carrots, celery and onion into a blender with 1 cup water. Process until smooth. Combine second cup of water and all remaining ingredients except butter in a saucepan and bring to a boil. Cover and simmer for 5 minutes. Remove from heat and stir in butter or oil.

STRACCIATELLA

6 servings

Add cooked chicken or shrimp for a one-dish meal.

2 cloves garlic
6 cups chicken broth
1 teaspoon salt, or to taste
6 cups shredded greens,
   such as cabbage, spinach
   or escarole

2 eggs
1/4 cup grated Parmesan cheese
1/2 cup seasoned croutons,
   homemade or purchased

Peel and split garlic. Add it to the stock and salt to taste. Bring to a boil, add greens and simmer for 5 minutes. Beat eggs with cheese. Just before serving, pour the egg mixture gradually into the simmering soup, stirring until the egg sets. Do not let soup boil. Top with croutons.

Mushroom Soup

6 servings

A simple soup elegant enough for the finest dinner party.

2 tablespoons olive oil	3 cups chicken broth
2 cloves garlic, chopped	¹/₂ teaspoon salt (optional)
1 pound mushrooms, sliced	¹/₂ teaspoon dried oregano
2 cups fresh tomatoes,	Salt and pepper, to taste
chopped	Grated Parmesan cheese (opt.)

Heat oil in a large saucepan. Sauté garlic and mushrooms for 5 minutes. Add remaining ingredients and bring to a boil. Cover and simmer 30 minutes. Add salt and pepper, to taste. Serve hot, sprinkled with grated Parmesan cheese, if desired.

Mom's Chicken Soup

8 servings

There's a wealth of health in this excellent version of Mom's traditional comfort food.

1 2 ¹/₂-pound chicken	3 cloves garlic, chopped
2 quarts water	Salt and pepper, to taste
2 carrots, sliced	1 cup uncooked rice or
2 stalks celery, sliced	noodles
1 medium onion, chopped	

The day before serving, simmer chicken, vegetables and spices in a large stock pot with the water and seasonings for 2 hours. Do not add rice. Let cool and remove chicken and vegetables. Set aside. Refrigerate broth, covered, overnight. In the meantime, skin and de-bone the chicken. Keep 2 cups chopped chicken meat for the soup and use the rest for other purposes. Save the vegetables in a covered container and refrigerate. The next day, 30 minutes before serving, skim the fat off the top of the broth and return the liquid to a large sauce pot. Add the reserved chicken chunks, vegetables and rice. Simmer for 30–40 minutes. If using noodles, add to pot 10–15 minutes before serving.

NOTE: The vegetables can be pureed in a blender with a little broth and added to the soup before serving to make it thicker. Or, you can stir in a cup of light cream.

FRESH TOMATO SOUP

4 servings

Here's a great way to use your bumper crop of fresh tomatoes. This soup can be frozen for 2 months. You can also add 1 cup of rice to the mixture to make it even more hearty.

2 tablespoons olive oil	4 cups chopped tomatoes
1 medium onion, chopped	1 tablespoon flour
2 cloves garlic, chopped	2 cups water
1 carrot, chopped	2 tablespoons fresh basil
1 stalk celery with leaves, chopped	Salt and freshly ground pepper, to taste

Heat the oil in a large saucepan. Add the onion, garlic, carrot and celery. Sauté for 5 minutes until onion becomes transparent.

Add tomatoes and simmer for 10 minutes, mashing occasionally with a wooden spoon until soft and pulpy. Sprinkle flour over the tomatoes and stir until smooth.

Add water and seasonings, bring to a boil, and simmer uncovered for 20 minutes. Puree the soup in a blender or food processor, if desired. Reheat before serving.

SENATE BEAN SOUP

6 servings

The soup that won raves in the U.S. Senate cafeteria gets a garlicky lift with this adaptation.

1 pound dried white beans
6 cups water or more
$\frac{1}{2}$ teaspoon crushed thyme
1 teaspoon oregano
$\frac{1}{2}$ pound potatoes
$\frac{1}{4}$ cup milk or light cream

$\frac{1}{2}$ cup each chopped celery
  and onion
2 cloves garlic, chopped
$\frac{1}{4}$ cup chopped fresh parsley
Salt and freshly ground pepper,
  to taste

Soak beans in water overnight. Drain. Cover beans with 6 cups of fresh water and bring to a boil in a large saucepan. Cover and simmer over low heat for 1 hour. Scrub potatoes and cut into thick slices. Steam or microwave until tender. Mash and add milk or cream until fluffy. Add potatoes and remaining ingredients to cooked beans. Cover and simmer gently for another hour, stirring occasionally and lightly mashing beans with a fork or potato masher until soup becomes pulpy. Add more water if needed. Taste for seasoning and serve warm.

MINESTRONE

6 servings

The Italians are famous for their frequent and flavorful use of garlic. This wonderful classic exemplifies how garlic adds that special touch of Italy to a meal-style soup. Don't be put off with the list of ingredients. Once you gather the goods, it's quite simple to put this soup together and well worth the effort.

2 cloves garlic, chopped
1 tablespoon olive oil
½ cup chopped onion
6 cups water
1 6-ounce can tomato paste
1 16-ounce can tomatoes
2 cups cooked white or
kidney beans
3 carrots, diced
2 stalks celery, sliced
½ pound potatoes, diced

1 teaspoon basil
1 teaspoon oregano
¼ cup chopped fresh parsley
1 cup uncooked pasta
(shells, elbows, rotini or
broken-up spaghetti)
2 cups shredded romaine or
spinach
Salt and freshly ground pepper,
to taste
Grated Parmesan (optional)

Sauté garlic briefly in oil over medium heat in a large stock pot or saucepan. Add the onion and cook for 5 minutes. Add the water, tomato paste, tomatoes, carrots, celery and potatoes and simmer, covered, for 30 minutes. Add the remaining ingredients and cook for 30 minutes more. Serve with grated Parmesan cheese and hot, crusty Italian bread.

GAZPACHO

4 servings

This cold soup of Spanish origin is a delight on hot, summer evenings as a first course. Or add crusty bread and you have a terrific light meal. Plain, low-fat yogurt or the new non-fat sour cream makes an excellent garnish.

2 cups cold water
1 large clove garlic, chopped
1 teaspoon salt
4 tablespoons olive oil
2 tablespoons wine vinegar
4 cups fresh tomatoes, chopped

3 tablespoons minced onion
½ teaspoon hot pepper sauce
or more, to taste
1 cup seasoned croutons,
for garnish

Blend all ingredients, except croutons, in a blender or food processor fitted with a steel blade. Marinate in the refrigerator for 1 hour. Serve chilled topped with croutons.

Cabbage Soup

6 servings

What can you say about a soup that combines the health-giving benefits of garlic with the anti-cancer fighter, cabbage? This delicious soup is hearty enough to serve as a complete meal in itself!

1 tablespoon oil
1 tablespoon butter
1 clove garlic
1 large onion, chopped
4 cups shredded cabbage
6 cups chicken or
   vegetable stock

2 tablespoons soy or
   tamari sauce
1 cup uncooked, long-grain rice
2 teaspoons salt, if stock
   is unsalted
$3/4$ cup grated cheese, any
   mixture is fine

Heat oil and butter in a large saucepan or stock pot. Peel and split garlic clove in half and add to the pot. Add onion and sauté until limp, about 5 minutes. Add cabbage to pot and stir to coat with fat. Cook 5 minutes more. Add stock and soy sauce. Bring mixture to a boil. Add rice, season if necessary, and cover pot. Lower heat and simmer for 30 minutes. Serve with grated cheese.

Yogurt Soup

4 servings

In the Middle East, this popular soup is often served with roast lamb or poultry. Fresh herbs really make a difference.

2 cups plain, low-fat yogurt
1 cup peeled, seeded,
   shredded cucumber
1 clove garlic, crushed

$1/4$ cup fresh mint or dill,
   chopped
Salt and freshly ground pepper,
   to taste

Beat all ingredients together with a wire whisk. Chill before serving. You can top each serving with a sprinkling of chopped nuts if desired.

VICHYSSOISE

8 servings

This classic potato-based soup is both refreshing and filling.

2 tablespoons olive oil	5 cups diced potatoes
or butter	1 quart chicken broth
1 cup chopped onion	$\frac{1}{2}$ cup nonfat dry milk powder
1 cup sliced leeks	Light cream, optional
2 cloves garlic, crushed	Salt and freshly ground pepper,
	to taste

Heat butter or oil in a large saucepan or stock pot. Sauté onion, leeks and garlic for 5 minutes or until soft. Add potatoes, broth and seasonings. Bring to a boil, cover and simmer for 25 minutes. Puree soup in a blender or food processor. Add nonfat milk powder and blend for 30 seconds. Chill and serve icy cold, blended with the additional cream just before serving. Sprinkle with chopped parsley.

Garlic is a *must* in most any salad dressing. Here are some of my favorite salads. The dressings are adaptable to any mixture of vegetables.

COUNTRY BEAN SALAD

4 servings

An excellent main dish or accompaniment to a buffet.

Salad:

1 16-ounce can three-bean salad, drained
1 15-ounce can chick peas
1 16-ounce can white potatoes
$\frac{1}{2}$ cup pickled beets
2 cups salad greens, washed and shredded
$\frac{1}{4}$ cup crumbled bacon or bacon bits

Dressing:

$\frac{1}{2}$ cup olive oil
$\frac{1}{4}$ cup wine vinegar
3 cloves garlic, crushed
1 teaspoon black pepper

Mix three bean salad with drained chick peas, potatoes and beets. Spoon over greens. Top with crumbled bacon. Thoroughly blend dressing ingredients. Drizzle dressing over all. Top with pepper.

GREEK COUNTRY SALAD

4 servings

I simply love this salad, not only because of my own Greek heritage but because it is the best main dish (or side salad) you can possibly have! Improvise, if you wish, by adding cooked shrimp, salmon or any other seafood. Serve with warm, crusty French, Greek or Italian bread or pita pockets. Chill the dinner plates for an hour before serving.

Salad:

4 cups shredded mixed greens
1 red onion, sliced
$\frac{1}{2}$ cup sliced, pickled beets
1 tomato, chopped
1 cucumber, sliced thinly

$\frac{1}{2}$ pound feta cheese, sliced
1 3$\frac{1}{2}$-ounce jar marinated
  artichoke hearts
  (keep the marinade)
6 black Kalamata olives

Dressing:

$\frac{1}{2}$ cup extra virgin olive oil
4 cloves garlic, minced
$\frac{1}{4}$ cup wine vinegar

1 teaspoon crushed oregano
  leaves
Salt and freshly ground
  pepper, to taste

Mix dressing (add the reserved artichoke oil) ingredients in a small jar and let stand. Arrange salad greens on a platter. Top with the remaining salad ingredients. Drizzle dressing over all.

Pasta Salad

4 servings

A great way to use leftover pasta. Spirals and shells work especially well in this main-dish salad that's also a good buffet dish with broiled chicken, roast beef or fish.

Salad:

- 2 cups cooked pasta
- 2 cups shredded salad greens
- 1 cup broccoli flowerets, lightly steamed
- 1 chopped tomato
- 1/4 cup each sliced black and green olives
- 4 ounces shredded cheddar cheese

Dressing:

- 1/2 cup olive oil
- 1/4 cup wine vinegar
- 1/2 cup low-fat yogurt
- 2 teaspoons fresh minced garlic
- 1 teaspoon black pepper
- 1 teaspoon fresh minced dill
- Salt and freshly ground pepper, to taste

Combine dressing ingredients. Toss pasta with dressing, salt and pepper to taste. Let stand to develop flavors. Arrange tomatoes and broccoli on top of pasta mixture. Sprinkle with olives and cheese. Serve chilled on salad greens.

FISH SALAD

1 serving

Use canned, drained salmon, shrimp or tuna for this excellent dinner salad that's great on warm summer evenings or when you aren't hungry enough for a heavy meal. This recipe serves one heartily and can be increased to serve many more. The garlic gives extra zip to the salmon, important when you are using canned instead of fresh fish.

1 6-ounce can fish
1 cup chopped celery
½ cup low-calorie
   mayonnaise
2 cloves garlic, crushed
½ cup finely chopped
   onion or scallions

¼ cup pimento stuffed
   olives, chopped
1 tomato, sliced
⅓ cucumber, peeled and sliced
2 cups shredded salad greens
Freshly ground pepper and
   paprika, to taste

Thoroughly combine first 6 ingredients. Arrange tomato and cucumber neatly on top of greens. Mound fish mixture in the center. Serve with sesame toast or pita bread.

CAESAR SALAD

4 servings

I don't know if Julius Caesar loved garlic, but this wonderful salad, that's a meal in itself, certainly gets its punch from lots of the bulb! I've left out the traditional raw egg for people with health concerns.

3 medium cloves garlic, crushed
$\frac{1}{4}$ teaspoon dry mustard
$\frac{1}{4}$ teaspoon salt
$\frac{1}{4}$ teaspoon ground pepper
$\frac{1}{2}$ cup extra virgin olive oil
2 tablespoons wine vinegar
$1\frac{1}{2}$ teaspoon Worcestershire sauce

8 anchovy fillets, drained and chopped
1 large head romaine lettuce, torn
$\frac{1}{2}$ cup grated Parmesan cheese
$1\frac{1}{2}$ tablespoons lemon juice
1 cup seasoned croutons

Combine the crushed garlic, mustard, salt, pepper, oil, vinegar, Worcestershire sauce and anchovies in a jar; cover and shake vigorously. Pour this dressing over the lettuce in a salad bowl. Add the cheese and toss the salad until it is well blended. Add the lemon juice and toss again. Add the croutons and toss gently; serve immediately.

SPINACH SALAD

4 servings

Another personal favorite! This one gets its bite from lots of fresh garlic.

Salad:

1 pound fresh spinach, washed and dried
½ cup bacon bits or fresh, crumbled cooked bacon
2 hard boiled eggs, sliced

½ pound mushrooms, washed and sliced thin
¼ cup sliced beets
Seasoned croutons to taste
¼ cup crumbled blue cheese (optional)

Dressing:

½ cup olive oil
5 cloves garlic, minced
¼ cup wine vinegar
Salt and freshly ground pepper, to taste

1 teaspoon Dijon-style mustard
1 teaspoon honey

Arrange spinach greens in a shallow bowl. Top with neatly arranged bacon bits, egg slices, mushrooms, beets, croutons and blue cheese. Blend dressing ingredients well. Drizzle over salad.

POTATO BROCCOLI SALAD

4 servings

This is an easy way to make good use of tender new potatoes.

Salad:

2 pounds steamed new
potatoes
3 cups steamed broccoli
flowerets
1/2 small red onion,
sliced into rings
1 small red pepper,
sliced into rings

Dressing:

1/4 cup wine or
cider vinegar
2 cloves garlic, peeled and
minced
Salt and freshly ground
pepper, to taste

Halve the potatoes and place on a serving plate with the broccoli in the center. Chill until serving time. Arrange the slices of onion and pepper neatly over the potato and broccoli mixture when ready to serve.

Combine the dressing ingredients in a small jar, shake well and pour over veggies.

CHRISTMAS SALAD

8 servings

This dish was a last-minute invention when we were invited to an unexpected holiday gathering. It was a festive hit!

Salad:
2 pints cherry tomatoes, washed
2 10-ounce packages of fresh or frozen Brussels sprouts, cooked for 4 minutes or until barely tender
½ pound feta cheese (or mozzarella), cut into cubes

Dressing:
½ cup olive oil
2 tablespoons wine vinegar
2 cloves garlic, minced
½ pound olives, pimento stuffed or black
Freshly ground black pepper, to taste

In an attractive serving bowl, combine tomatoes and sprouts. Top with chunks of feta and olives. Mix dressing ingredients well and drizzle over the salad. Top with a grinding of fresh pepper.

TABBOULEH

10 appetizer servings

This Middle Eastern dish is always a welcome addition to any buffet table.

Salad:

1 cup bulgur
1 cup tomato sauce
1 cup chicken broth

3 firm tomatoes, chopped
1 cup fresh parsley, chopped
½ cup chopped scallions

Dressing:

½ cup fresh lemon juice
2 tablespoons olive oil

2 teaspoons minced fresh garlic
Freshly ground pepper, to taste

Place the bulgur in a medium-sized casserole. Heat the tomato sauce and broth to boiling and pour the liquid over the bulgur, stirring once. Let stand for one hour.

Drain off excess liquid and chill bulgur until serving time. Mix dressing and pour over the bulgur. Toss well and let stand one hour before serving to let flavors blend. Bring to room temperature.

CARROT SALAD

4 servings

This is not your wimpy version of a mayonnaise-laced salad! It's a North African recipe that's spicy and delicious.

1 pound carrots, julienned	1 teaspoon honey
$\frac{1}{2}$ cup raisins	1 teaspoon cumin
$\frac{1}{4}$ cup fresh lemon juice	$\frac{1}{4}$ cup chopped parsley
1 teaspoon olive oil	Freshly ground black
2 tablespoons minced garlic	pepper, to taste

Place carrots in a bowl with the raisins and combine the remaining ingredients in a small jar or bowl. Pour the dressing over the carrots and raisins, tossing to mix well. Let stand one hour before serving.

Vegetables take on a new dimension when kissed with garlic. Ordinary green beans, for example, develop a subtle flavor that's quite remarkable. Stir-fried veggies are both healthy and tasty when sautéed in garlic infused oil. Try some of these easy and garlicky vegetables for your family and friends. You'll be surprised how even diehard antivegetable eaters perk up when garlic adds its magic touch.

VEGETABLE STIR FRY

4 servings

Any combination of vegetables will taste good cooked this way. Just make sure to cut them into small pieces on a diagonal for maximum cooking surface.

1 cup each carrots, celery and zucchini, sliced on the diagonal
½ cup each broccoli and cauliflower flowerets
2 tablespoons olive oil

3 cloves garlic, minced
¼ cup dry white wine or chicken broth
1 tablespoon soy or tamari sauce
1 tablespoon lemon juice

Heat oil to 350° in a non-stick pan. Add vegetables and stir to coat with the oil. Add garlic and stir fry for 5 minutes. Add the remaining ingredients, stir and simmer the mixture, covered, for 2 minutes more. Serve immediately for maximum flavor and nutrition.

GARLICKY CARROTS

4 servings

A simple but delicious dish that raises the lowly carrot to lofty elegance!

1 pound carrots, sliced
   into 1-inch pieces
6 cloves fresh garlic,
   peeled and sliced

$1/4$ cup water
2 tablespoons butter
Salt and freshly ground
   pepper, to taste

Place carrots and garlic in a large saucepan. Add water and cook over medium heat until just done, about 5 minutes.

Add butter and seasonings, stir to melt and coat.

GREEK CAULIFLOWER

6 servings

This flavorful dish enhances any seafood or poultry dish.

1 head cauliflower
2 tablespoons extra
   virgin olive oil
2 tablespoons minced garlic

2 tablespoons chopped parsley
Salt and freshly ground pepper,
   to taste

Separate cauliflower into flowerets and cook or steam just until tender. Heat the oil in a small frying pan and cook garlic and parsley for 2 minutes. Add salt and pepper to taste. Pour over the warm cauliflower and serve with additional chopped parsley if desired.

Eggplant with Garlic

4 servings

Eggplant, that beautiful purple-hued vegetable, and garlic make a wonderful marriage of flavors! Here is a favorite dish that we prepare quite often.

1 eggplant, sliced into
 $\frac{1}{2}$ -inch slices
1 egg, beaten
2 cloves garlic, peeled and
 sliced thinly

$\frac{1}{2}$ cup olive oil
1 cup seasoned
 bread crumbs
$\frac{1}{4}$ cup grated Parmesan
 cheese

Preheat oven to 350°.

Dip eggplant slices, one at a time, in the beaten egg. Now coat with seasoned bread crumbs and lay flat on a platter. Refrigerate the coated slices for 1 hour. Meanwhile, prepare garlic. In a large frying pan, add the oil and heat just until smoking. Add the garlic and fry the eggplant slices over medium-high heat until brown on each side, about 5 minutes per side. Drain on paper towels.

Place the fried slices into an oiled, rectangular casserole. Arrange neatly and sprinkle with grated cheese. Bake for 15 minutes.

Eggplant Stew

4 servings

A quick version of ratatouille.

$\frac{1}{4}$ cup olive oil
1 eggplant, peeled
 and cubed
4 cloves garlic, chopped
1 onion, chopped
2 medium zucchini,
 sliced thickly

2 carrots, sliced thinly
2 cups chicken broth
2 cups tomato puree
$\frac{1}{4}$ cup wine vinegar
2 teaspoons dried oregano
Salt and freshly ground pepper,
 to taste

In a large saucepan, heat the oil and add eggplant cubes, garlic and onion. Sauté for 5 minutes, stirring frequently. Add the remaining ingredients except the vinegar. Bring mixture to a boil, cover, and simmer for 20 minutes. Stir in wine vinegar and adjust seasonings.

NOTE: You can add sliced cooled potatoes, cooked and drained sausage or other varieties of green vegetables to the stew.

AMAZING BROCCOLI

6 servings

I'm sure even George Bush, known for his dislike of broccoli, would adore this vitamin-rich vegetable prepared with a healthy dose of garlic! Serve cold with a garlic-laced mayonnaise or dip.

1 pound fresh broccoli, cut into flowerets and stems	$^1/_4$ cup wine vinegar
5 cloves garlic, crushed	2 tablespoons olive oil
	1 teaspoon salt

Place all ingredients in a large sauce pot. Cook until broccoli is just tender, about 5 minutes. Refrigerate several hours before serving.

BROCCOLI CASSEROLE

6 servings

An unusual way to prepare this popular vegetable that's sure to please even the most finicky eater.

1/2 cup chopped onion
1/4 cup olive oil
2 tablespoons chopped garlic
1 pound broccoli, steamed until tender

1 cup seasoned bread crumbs
1/2 cup grated Parmesan cheese
1 egg, beaten
Salt and freshly ground pepper, to taste

Preheat oven to 300°.

Sauté onion in the oil. Stir in garlic, broccoli, bread crumbs and cheese. Blend well. Add egg and blend again. Adjust seasoning to taste and place mixture into a shallow buttered casserole. Bake for 20 minutes.

GARLIC GREEN BEANS

4 servings

Green beans are always plentiful and inexpensive. Here's an excellent way to make ordinary beans sizzle with flavor.

1 pound green beans, washed, trimmed and cut into 2-inch pieces
2 tablespoons butter
1 small onion, chopped

3 cloves garlic, minced
1 8-ounce can tomato sauce
1 teaspoon dried oregano
Salt and freshly ground pepper, to taste

Steam beans for 5 minutes until tender-crisp. Place in a serving dish and set aside. Fry onion and garlic in the butter in a small frying pan over medium heat for 3 minutes. Add tomato sauce and seasonings. Cook 5 minutes more. Pour over beans and toss thoroughly to blend flavors.

GARLIC MUSHROOMS

4 servings

A super-satisfying dish that couldn't be easier to make. Perfect for dinner parties!

1 pound sliced mushrooms	4 tablespoons chopped
4 tablespoons olive oil	fresh parsley
6 cloves fresh garlic, sliced	Salt and freshly ground pepper, to taste

In a large skillet, sauté mushrooms in olive oil for 5 minutes. Add garlic, parsley, salt and pepper to taste. Simmer over medium heat, covered, 5 minutes more. Serve with roast chicken or lamb.

GARLIC SPUDS

4 servings

This unusual recipe is a sure-fire hit.

4 baking potatoes, peeled	$\frac{1}{2}$ cup light cream
$\frac{1}{2}$ teaspoon salt	2 tablespoons butter or margarine
$\frac{1}{2}$ onion, sliced	$\frac{1}{2}$ cup grated cheddar cheese
4 cups water	for garnish
3 cloves fresh garlic, peeled	

Boil potatoes, onion and garlic in salted water until soft. Drain off the water but reserve the onion and garlic. Mash the mixture with a fork or potato masher. Add light cream and butter, beat well. Sprinkle with grated cheese.

SPINACH CASSEROLE

6 servings

A tasty casserole that's great for company.

2 pounds fresh spinach
1 cup ricotta cheese
1 pound cottage cheese
4 large eggs, well beaten
2 teaspoons minced fresh
   garlic

$1/2$ teaspoon nutmeg
Lots of fresh black pepper
1 tablespoon lemon juice
Dash of paprika for
   the topping
1 cup fresh bread crumbs

Preheat oven to 375°.

In a large skillet, cook fresh spinach over medium heat, stirring until it wilts. Remove from heat, and blend with remaining ingredients, except bread crumbs.

Spread into a buttered 9-x-13-inch pan. Sprinkle with bread crumbs and dust with paprika. Bake, covered, for 20 minutes. Uncover and cook 10 minutes more.

TERRIFIC TOMATOES

Simply irresistible is how guests describe this colorful dish!

4 tomatoes, sliced
3 cloves garlic, minced
5 scallions, minced
2 tablespoons chopped
   parsley

$1/3$ cup olive oil
$1/4$ cup wine vinegar
1 teaspoon oregano
Salt and freshly ground pepper,
   to taste

Preheat oven to 350°

Arrange the tomatoes on a platter. Mix garlic, scallions and parsley. Sprinkle over the tomatoes. Prepare dressing by mixing oil, vinegar and oregano. Drizzle over sliced tomatoes. Marinate 30 minutes before serving.

POTATO CURRY

6 servings

This adaptation of a Tibetan dish comes from my dear friend, Jacqueline Keeley, who worked and taught in Tibet for a decade.

4 pounds unpeeled Idaho potatoes, cooked
$\frac{1}{2}$ cup chopped tomato
3 large cloves garlic, minced
$\frac{1}{2}$ teaspoon ginger

$\frac{1}{2}$ teaspoon ground coriander
$\frac{1}{2}$ teaspoon curry powder
2 tablespoons olive oil
Salt and freshly ground pepper, to taste

Peel cooled potatoes and cut them into $\frac{1}{2}$-inch diced pieces. Put them into a glass serving bowl. In a blender, combine tomato, garlic, ginger, coriander, curry and olive oil. Blend well and toss with the potatoes. Season with salt and pepper. Serve at room temperature.

GARLIC PEAS AND RICE

6 servings

Use aromatic basmati rice for this flavorful dish.

1 teaspoon olive oil
2 cloves garlic, minced
1 medium onion, chopped
1 teaspoon curry powder

2 cups basmati rice
4 cups water
2 cups frozen peas
1 cup diced green pepper

Heat the oil in a large saucepan and add onion and garlic. Sauté for 5 minutes and add curry powder, rice and water. Bring to a boil and simmer, covered, for 40 minutes or until rice is tender. Add the peas and pepper and cook 5 minutes more.

CRUSTY POTATOES WITH GARLIC OIL

6 servings

This inexpensive but sumptuous dish may be simple fare, but to me and my family, it's delicious!

6 medium potatoes,
   peeled and sliced thinly
3 large onions, thinly sliced
4 garlic cloves, minced
1 28-ounce can plum
   tomatoes, drained
   and chopped

½ cup olive oil
2 teaspoons oregano
Salt and freshly ground
   pepper, to taste

Preheat the oven to 400°. In a large bowl, combine the potatoes, onions, garlic and tomatoes. Pour the olive oil and sprinkle oregano over the mixture and toss to coat well.

Add salt and pepper to taste. Spread into a shallow baking dish and cover tightly with foil. Bake 30 minutes. Remove foil and bake 40 minutes longer or until the potatoes are tender.

There is a growing awareness of the health benefits of pasta, grains and rice in our North American diet. Many experts believe that we eat too much animal protein with far too much fat. In this section, we feature a variety of low-fat, healthy recipes that rely on non-animal products to produce wonderful meals.

This first recipe, a quick version of ravioli and garlic with fresh vegetables, is an excellent example of how you can feed your family economically and in short order.

RAVIOLI WITH GARLIC-TOMATO SAUCE

4-6 servings

1 pound fresh or frozen ravioli	1 10-ounce can stewed tomatoes
$1/4$ cup olive or canola oil	1 teaspoon oregano
3 garlic cloves, minced	Freshly ground pepper, to taste
3 medium peppers, cored and sliced into strips	$1/4$ cup grated Parmesan cheese

Preheat oven to 350°.

Bring a large pot of salted water to a boil and cook the ravioli for 10 minutes. Drain and place in a greased 2-quart casserole. In a large skillet, heat the oil over medium heat and add the garlic. Sauté for 2 minutes.

Add the peppers and tomatoes; add the oregano and pepper. Simmer for 5 minutes. Pour sauce over ravioli. Sprinkle on the cheese and heat in the oven until serving time.

LOW-FAT MARINARA SAUCE

Makes 2 ½ cups

1 tablespoon olive oil
1 small onion, chopped fine
2 cloves garlic, chopped
1 green pepper, cored,
   seeded and chopped fine

1 teaspoon oregano
1 teaspoon black pepper
2 cups tomato sauce

Heat oil in a medium saucepan over low heat. Add onion and garlic and sauté for 5 minutes. Add remaining ingredients and simmer for 15 minutes. Serve over pasta, chicken or seafood.

NEW AGE CREAM SAUCE

Makes 2 ½ cups

I love this sauce that I developed to use over cooked pasta, vegetables and just about anything I used to smother with cream sauce! It's even good over baked potatoes topped with cooked spinach.

2 tablespoons low-calorie
   margarine
2 tablespoons flour
2 teaspoons minced garlic

2 cups chicken broth
½ cup skim milk
2 tablespoons grated
   Parmesan cheese

In a small saucepan over low heat, melt margarine. Stir in flour until smooth. Gradually add garlic and chicken broth, cooking over medium heat until the mixture starts to boil and becomes thick. Stir frequently to prevent lumps. When sauce is thick, lower heat and gradually add milk. Stir. Add cheese just before serving.

NOTE: You can also cook this in a microwave safe measuring cup for four minutes on high, stirring every minute or so.

EGGPLANT SAUCE

Makes 3 cups

This is great for pasta, noodles, rice or polenta—that corn meal mixture that's a favorite in Italian cuisine. You can also use this sauce, with a little water or chicken broth added, to simmer chicken pieces into a wonderfully aromatic stew.

2 tablespoons olive oil
3 garlic cloves, minced
½ teaspoon red pepper flakes
1 28-ounce can of tomato
    puree
2 teaspoons red wine vinegar

1 medium eggplant,
    peeled and cubed
1 green pepper, cored,
    seeded and diced
2 cups sliced mushrooms
Salt and freshly ground pepper,
    to taste

Heat the oil in a large skillet and sauté the garlic for a minute. Add red pepper flakes, tomato puree, vinegar, salt and pepper.

Bring to a boil. Add the eggplant and simmer 10 minutes, stirring occasionally. Add the pepper and mushrooms and simmer 10 minutes more. Let cool and refrigerate overnight to develop flavors.

ANGEL HAIR PASTA WITH CLAMS

2 servings

1 10-ounce jar whole
    clams
Reserved clam juice, plus
    enough water or
    white wine to make 1 cup
2 teaspoons cornstarch
6 ounces angel hair pasta,
    also called capellini

1 tablespoon olive oil
1 tablespoon margarine
2 scallions, sliced
2 large garlic cloves, minced
Salt and freshly ground pepper,
    to taste
1 teaspoon oregano
3 tablespoons chopped parsley

Drain the clams, reserving 1 cup juice. Add cornstarch to the juice with water or wine and blend well. Cook the capellini according to the package directions. Do not overcook. Drain and reserve. Meanwhile, heat oil and margarine in a pan; add the scallions, garlic, salt and pepper. Cook for 3 minutes. Add oregano, clams and the clam-cornstarch mixture. Stir over low heat until mixture thickens. Add the parsley, turn up the heat, and bring the sauce to a boil. Serve immediately over drained pasta.

EASY VEGETABLE LASAGNA

8 servings

A meatless variation of a popular favorite that is easily prepared in your microwave oven.

1 pound mushrooms, sliced
1 large onion, chopped
4 cloves garlic, minced
1 10-ounce package frozen chopped spinach, defrosted and drained well
1 pound cottage cheese
$^1/_2$ pound feta cheese, crumbled

$^1/_2$ cup grated Parmesan cheese
1 teaspoon oregano
4 cups tomato or commercial spaghetti sauce
1 pound lasagna noodles
8 ounces shredded skim mozzarella cheese

Preheat oven to 350°.

Combine mushrooms, onions and garlic in bowl. Cover and microwave for 3 minutes on high. Combine cottage cheese, feta cheese, and half the Parmesan with the oregano in another bowl.

In a microwavable lasagna pan, layer sauce, noodles, cheese mixture, spinach, mushroom/onion mixture. Repeat until all these ingredients are gone. Top with mozzarella cheese.

Cover with double plastic wrap. Refrigerate overnight.

Remove pan one hour before baking. Microwave on high for 5 minutes. Microwave on medium 30 minutes more. Let stand 5 minutes before serving. Sprinkle remaining Parmesan over the casserole.

NOTE: To cook conventionally, do not cover with plastic wrap. Bake, covered with foil, 60 minutes or until bubbly. Uncover for 15 more minutes.

PASTA PRIMAVERA

3 servings

Any variety of vegetables is great. Frozen vegetables make this an easy dish to make.

$1/2$ pound pasta, such as shells, bows, rotini or elbows	1 16-ounce package frozen mixed Italian vegetables
1 tablespoon oil	2 cups New Age Cream Sauce (See page 84)
4 cloves fresh garlic, cut into slivers	2 tablespoons grated Parmesan cheese
Dash salt	

Fill a large kettle or 5-quart saucepan with at least 2 quarts water. Add a dash of salt and bring to a rolling boil. Add pasta and boil for 8 minutes. In the meantime, make New Age Cream Sauce and set aside. In a large skillet sauté vegetables in hot oil for 5 minutes. Drain pasta and toss with vegetables. Pour New Age Cream Sauce over pasta and toss well. Sprinkle with grated cheese and serve immediately on warm dinner plates.

SHRIMP SCAMPI WITH PASTA

4 servings

A low-fat dish that combines sumptuous shrimp and pasta laced with garlicky flavor.

1 pound fettucini	2 tablespoons chopped scallions
2 cups chicken broth	4 tablespoons chopped parsley
2 tablespoons chopped garlic	1 pound peeled, deveined shrimp
	Salt and freshly ground pepper, to taste

Cook pasta according to package directions. Combine broth, garlic, scallions and parsley in a large saucepan. Bring to a boil and simmer, uncovered, 3 minutes.

Add shrimp to broth. Simmer 5 minutes or until shrimp turns pink. Pour mixture over drained, warm pasta. Serve immediately.

RICE AND GARLIC

4 servings

Use this basic recipe and add your own imagination. A can of beans, corn, cooked spinach and even shrimp or tuna are excellent additions. I make this in my microwave, but you can cook the rice conventionally if you prefer.

1 cup long-grain rice	2 teaspoons lemon juice
2 cups chicken or beef broth	2 teaspoons olive oil
2 tablespoons minced garlic	

Place all ingredients in a microwavable casserole large enough that the mixture only fills halfway. Mix well. Cover with plastic wrap and turn back a corner or edge to allow steam to escape.

Microwave on high for 5 minutes. Reduce power to medium-low and cook for 18 more minutes. Fluff with a fork.

NOTE: For brown rice, increase the second cooking time on medium low to 40 minutes.

PASTA WITH SAUSAGE

4 servings

A real Italian treat! Any pasta will do, but shells or noodles are great.

½ pound pasta	½ pound sliced sausage
2 teaspoons olive oil	(turkey, veal or pork)
½ sliced onion	1 cup tomato or
4 cloves garlic, cut	spaghetti sauce
into slivers	1 teaspoon black pepper
½ pound sliced	½ cup grated Parmesan
mushrooms	cheese

Heat 3 quarts water in a 5-quart saucepan. In the meantime, place the remaining ingredients (except pasta and cheese) in a large skillet. Cook, stirring, over medium heat.

When the water boils in the saucepan, add the pasta. Cook uncovered for 10 minutes. Drain the pasta in a colander. Place the pasta in a heated serving bowl. Toss with the sauce ingredients in the skillet, mixing well. Top with cheese and serve on warm dinner plates.

LOW-FAT NOODLES ALFREDO

4 servings

An updated version of a usually high-calorie, high-fat pasta dish.

1 pound pasta	2 cloves garlic, chopped
1 pound low-fat, creamy	Salt and freshly ground
cottage cheese	pepper, to taste
1 cup tomato sauce	1 large, ripe tomato, diced
¼ cup grated	1 cup fresh basil or
Parmesan cheese	¼ cup chopped fresh basil
2 tablespoons skim milk	leaves

Cook pasta according to package directions. Meanwhile, mix cottage cheese, tomato sauce, Parmesan cheese, milk, garlic, salt and pepper in the blender until smooth.

Drain pasta and place in a warm serving casserole or skillet. Toss with cheese mixture and top with tomatoes and chopped basil.

NOODLE PUDDING

6 servings

This excellent recipe comes from Roz Suss, a South Florida cook who specializes in traditional Jewish cuisine.

½ pound broad noodles	1 teaspoon minced garlic
3 eggs, beaten	Dash of cinnamon
½ cup sugar	1 teaspoon vanilla
½ pound cottage cheese	1 cup low-fat milk
½ pint sour cream	1 cup noodle water
¼ cup butter, melted	1 cup raisins

Preheat oven to 350°.

Boil noodles and drain. Place noodles in bowl and mix with remaining ingredients. Place mixture into a well-greased 13-x-9-inch pan. Bake, uncovered, for 1½ hours.

STUFFED TOMATOES WITH COUSCOUS

4 servings

One of the best of the vegetarian cookbooks is *Quick Vegetarian Pleasures* by Jeanne Lemlin. Her collection of recipes is eclectic but easy to prepare. Here is a favorite summer dish that makes liberal use of fresh garlic. I've adapted Lemlin's recipe to trim time even further.

4 large, ripe tomatoes	1 cup frozen peas, thawed
1 cup couscous	1 cup shredded
1½ cups boiling	mozzarella cheese
chicken broth	1 teaspoon dried oregano
¼ cup oil or margarine	Salt and freshly ground pepper,
3 cloves garlic, minced	to taste

Preheat oven to 375°.

Slice the top off the tomatoes and scoop out the insides. Reserve the pulp for another use. Turn over the tomatoes and let them drain on paper towels.

Make the stuffing by pouring the chicken broth over the couscous and let stand, covered, for 10 minutes. Heat the oil in a frying pan and sauté the garlic and peas. Place the tomatoes in a shallow glass pan.

When the garlic and peas are coated with oil, add them to the couscous along with the remaining ingredients. Fluff lightly with a fork and gently stuff the tomatoes with the couscous mixture. Bake 30 minutes, basting occasionally with the pan juices.

P O U L T R Y

Garlic enhances any bird, adding a tantalizing aroma and a delicate taste. In the following recipes, you can interchange boneless, skinless chicken breast with turkey cutlets.

TERIYAKI CHICKEN

4 servings

This is a household favorite—a low-cal standby that's good any time of the year, but especially during the hot summer months when nobody feels like cooking indoors.

1 chicken, cut up and skin removed	¹/₂ cup teriyaki sauce (see page 113 for home-made teriyaki sauce)
2 cloves garlic, chopped	
1 green onion, chopped	

Rub garlic into chicken. Sprinkle with green onion. Pour teriyaki sauce over chicken. Cover tightly and refrigerate at least 4 hours, turning chicken pieces frequently. Broil on an outdoor grill or in the oven 5 inches from the heat source for 15 to 20 minutes turning twice or until there is no pink left in the juices when pierced with a fork.

NOTE: Budget-wise, chicken legs are your best bet these days. Skin chicken legs and freeze them, already marinated in a freezer bag for later use.

ð   ð   ð   ð

HONEY MUSTARD CHICKEN BREASTS

4 servings

This is a dish I truly treasure. It's delicious and very simple to prepare. Serve with steamed rice and spinach.

2 pounds boneless, skinless chicken breasts
1/4 cup honey
2 tablespoons prepared mustard
1 tablespoon soy sauce
1 tablespoon minced fresh garlic

Mix honey, mustard, soy sauce and garlic. Pour over chicken breasts and cover tightly in a food storage bag or in a microwavable dish, covered with plastic wrap. Marinate in the refrigerator for several hours or overnight.

One hour before serving, remove the chicken from the fridge and let stand at room temperature. Microwave, covered with vented plastic wrap for 15 minutes on medium high, turning twice. Cook until done.

NOTE: You can also fry the chicken breasts in a non-stick pan for 5 minutes each side.

BREADED CHICKEN BREASTS WITH CHEESE

4 servings

This lovely, easy dish is delicious with steamed Brussels sprouts or broccoli, cooked with fresh garlic, of course!

2 whole boneless, skinless chicken breasts
2 tablespoons seasoned flour or bread crumbs
1 tablespoon margarine or olive oil
2 slices mozzarella cheese
1 teaspoon garlic powder or granulated garlic

Dip the chicken breasts in bread crumbs or flour to cover. Heat oil or margarine in a large skillet and brown breasts on both sides, about 4 minutes each side. Top with slices of cheese and sprinkle with garlic. Lower heat, and simmer 10 minutes more. Serve over hot noodles.

NOTE: The mozzarella can be omitted or replaced with 1/2 cup grated Parmesan cheese.

🐜 🐜 🐜 🐜

LEMON HERB CHICKEN

4 servings

You can easily double, triple or even quadruple this recipe!

4 chicken leg quarters,
  skin removed
1 tablespoon olive oil
1 tablespoon fresh lemon
  juice

1 teaspoon oregano
1 clove garlic, minced

Mix lemon juice, spices and garlic for the marinade.

Pour marinade over chicken. Cover with plastic wrap and chill for at least 2 hours, turning chicken over twice. Preheat oven to 350°. Place leg quarters in a casserole large enough to hold them in a single layer and bake for 20 to 30 minutes, turning the legs over once.

CHINESE CHICKEN BREASTS

4 servings

An easy dish that tastes exotic.

1 teaspoon sesame oil
2 whole boneless, skinless
  chicken breasts
2 cloves garlic, minced
$\frac{1}{4}$ cup chopped onion

2 cups broccoli flowerets
1 10-ounce package frozen
  snow pea pods
  (fresh are even better)
$\frac{1}{4}$ cup soy sauce
$\frac{1}{2}$ cup dry white wine

Heat the oil in a large skillet. Add chicken breasts and brown on both sides. Add garlic, onion, broccoli, snow pea pods, soy sauce and wine, stir. Cover and simmer for 10 minutes. Serve over steamed rice.

Roast Chicken

4 servings

Adding slivers of fresh garlic to any roast elevates a simple meal to one fit for a king—or queen! Use a sharp knife and cut holes all over the bird. Then, insert slivers of fresh garlic into the slits.

    1 3-pound roasting chicken
    2 whole garlic cloves, cut into thin slivers
    Salt and freshly ground pepper, to taste
    2 medium potatoes, cut into quarters
    4 carrots, cut into 1-inch pieces
    1 onion, cut into quarters
    1/4 cup water or wine

Preheat oven to 350°.

Clean the chicken under running water. Trim away all excess fat. Make small slits in the chicken skin. Insert garlic into slits. Sprinkle seasoning over the bird.

Surround the chicken with vegetables. Add 1/4 cup wine or water. Cover loosely with foil and cook for 45 minutes. Remove foil and cook 15 minutes longer or until the bird is browned and the veggies are tender-crisp.

Curried Chicken

4 servings

This dish has an Indian heritage and a very special exotic flavor. It is delicious served with brown or white rice.

    1 small chicken, skinned and cut into serving pieces
    1 cup plain, non-fat yogurt
    3 cloves garlic, crushed
    1 teaspoon curry powder
    2 tablespoons oil

Place the chicken pieces in a bowl. In another smaller bowl, combine the yogurt, curry and garlic. Toss the chicken with the yogurt mixture and coat well. Cover the bowl and refrigerate overnight.

Remove chicken pieces from marinade. Heat oil in an electric skillet at 400°. Brown chicken well on all sides. Add reserved marinade to skillet. Stir and cover. Reduce heat and simmer for 30 minutes.

MOCK CHICKEN CACCIATORE

4 servings

This is a streamlined version of one of my all-time favorite dishes. I used to prepare it with whole, cut-up chicken—with the skin left on! Here's an up-to-date version to fit today's health conscious and busy lifestyle.

1 10-ounce package frozen chopped spinach, thawed and drained
2 teaspoons oil for frying
2 cloves garlic, chopped
$\frac{1}{2}$ cup chopped onion
4 skinless chicken breast halves, with bone
1 pound sliced mushrooms
1 16-ounce can stewed tomatoes
1 teaspoon oregano
Salt and freshly ground pepper, to taste

Preheat an electric skillet to 350°.

Heat oil in skillet, add garlic and onion. Add chicken breasts and brown on each side. Add mushrooms. Stir for 3 minutes. Add tomatoes, spinach and spices. Cover the skillet and cook for 10 more minutes. Serve over hot-cooked noodles or with French or Cuban bread.

SHEPHERD'S PIE

4–6 servings

A crustless version of a popular favorite that uses garlic in a very subtle way.

1 pound ground turkey	1 teaspoon Worcestershire
½ cup onions,	sauce
chopped fine	1 teaspoon steak sauce
2 cloves garlic, minced	½ cup dry red wine or water
1 1-ounce package dry	½ cup instant mashed potato
onion soup mix	flakes
½ cup ketchup	

Preheat oven to 350°.

Brown turkey, onions and garlic in a large non-stick frying pan over medium-low heat until all pink disappears. Mix in remaining ingredients and combine very well. Stir to break up any lumps. Simmer for 5 minutes.

Place mixture into a Pyrex or oven-proof pie plate. Cover with foil wrap. Bake for 20 minutes. Uncover and bake 10 minutes more. Serve with a green salad and corn on the cob.

TURKEY CUTLETS FRANÇAISE

4–5 servings

Another dish from my dear friend, Roz Suss, who also believes that flavorful food need not be time consuming nor fattening.

2 eggs, beaten	2 cloves garlic, peeled
Salt and pepper	and sliced
2 ½ pounds turkey	Juice of ½ lemon
cutlets, pounded thin	1 cup chicken broth
½ cup flour	¼ cup white wine
¼ cup oil	6 tablespoons butter

Mix salt and pepper into beaten eggs. Dip cutlets into the flour, then into the egg, and then back into the flour. Set aside. Heat oil in a 12-inch non-stick skillet. Add the garlic slices. Fry the cutlets on both sides until brown. Drain well on paper towels . Sauté for 2 minutes. Clean skillet and add butter; melt over low heat.

Add lemon, broth and wine and return cutlets to skillet. Simmer for 15 minutes, covered. Sprinkle with parsley before serving.

TURKEY DIVAN

4 servings

An excellent way to use leftover turkey—or chicken.

8 slices cooked turkey or 2 cups leftover chopped turkey
2 10-ounce packages frozen broccoli spears, thawed
1 10-ounce can cream of mushroom soup
1 soup can low-fat milk
1 teaspoon each garlic granules and white pepper
$\frac{1}{2}$ cup shredded Swiss or mozzarella cheese
Hot, cooked rice or noodles

Preheat oven to 350°.

Place turkey in a shallow casserole. Top with broccoli spears. Mix soup and milk. Pour over casserole. Sprinkle on spices. Bake, covered, for 30 minutes. Top with shredded cheese and heat 15 minutes more, uncovered. Serve with rice or noodles.

ROAST TURKEY OR TURKEY BREAST

Prepare the same way as you would roast chicken (page 94), but adjust cooking times to the size of your bird. Allow 20 minutes per pound in a conventional oven and 10 to 12 minutes per pound in the microwave. Remember to turn the bird over halfway through for even cooking.

Turkey Jambalaya

4 servings

Garlic gives this easy but elegant dish extra richness and flavor.

2 teaspoons sesame oil
4 cloves garlic, peeled
   and cut in halves
1 pound turkey cutlets,
   cut into strips
1 onion, chopped
1 green pepper, chopped
$\frac{1}{2}$ cup celery
$\frac{1}{2}$ pound turkey sausage,
   chopped

$\frac{1}{2}$ cup long-grain rice
1 cup chicken broth
1 cup tomato sauce or
   tomato puree
$\frac{1}{2}$ pound frozen shrimp
1 10-ounce package frozen peas
$\frac{1}{2}$ pound mushrooms, sliced
Salt and freshly ground pepper,
   to taste
1 teaspoon paprika

Preheat electric skillet to 350°.

Add oil, and when it sizzles, add garlic halves, turkey cutlets, onion, green pepper, celery, sausage and rice. Stir and cook for 3 to 5 minutes. Add the broth and tomato sauce. Cover and reduce heat to 300°. Cook for 15 minutes or until almost all of the liquid is absorbed. Add the remaining ingredients. Stir and cook 5 minutes longer, adding more broth if necessary.

Turkey Chili and Macaroni

4–6 servings

A new slant on an old favorite!

1 pound ground turkey
1 16-ounce can stewed
   tomatoes
2 cups tomato sauce
1 cup chopped onion
3 cloves garlic, minced
1 teaspoon chili powder
1 teaspoon oregano

Freshly ground pepper,
   to taste
1 16-ounce can kidney,
   beans, drained and rinsed
2 cups frozen mixed
   vegetables, thawed
$\frac{1}{2}$ lb elbow macaroni,
   cooked al dente and drained

Put turkey into a large, non-stick frying pan or electric skillet. Cook, stirring, over medium heat until all traces of pink disappear. Add tomatoes, tomato sauce, onion, garlic and seasonings. Simmer, covered, for 20 minutes.

Add the beans and vegetables. Simmer, covered, 10 minutes more. Add the cooked macaroni and heat thoroughly before serving. Serve with a mixed green salad and rolls.

MEAT DISHES

Be creative in preparing even plain, broiled steaks and chops. Buy cuts that look lean and then trim excess visible fat before cooking. Let garlic—not unhealthy fat—add the flavor.

TENNESSEE CHILI

6–8 servings

2 tablespoons vegetable oil
2 cloves garlic, minced
1 large onion, chopped
1 pound lean ground beef
2 tablespoons chili powder
$\frac{1}{2}$ teaspoon salt

1 28-ounce can whole tomatoes
2 28-ounce cans kidney beans, drained and rinsed
Chopped scallions
Grated cheese
Chopped tomatoes

Heat oil in a 3-quart saucepan over medium-high heat. Add garlic and onion and cook 3 minutes, stirring frequently. Add ground beef and cook, stirring, until the meat loses its pink color. Stir in spices. Add tomatoes with their liquid and bring to a boil, stirring and breaking up the tomatoes with a back of a spoon. Reduce heat to low and cook 10 minutes until mixture thickens, stirring occasionally. Add beans, stir and heat for 3 minutes longer. Serve with chopped scallions, grated Cheddar cheese and chopped, fresh tomatoes for garnish.

🐚 🐚 🐚 🐚

RUMP ROAST

8 servings

This lean cut can be easily prepared—if you are patient. To serve, slice thinly against the grain.

1 5-pound rump roast	1 cup red wine or water
1 1-ounce package onion soup mix	1 onion, quartered
2 tablespoons minced fresh garlic	4 carrots, scraped and left whole
$\frac{1}{2}$ cup ketchup	4 small red potatoes, washed and scrubbed

Preheat oven to 325°.

Place the roast in a large casserole or roasting pan. Sprinkle with soup mix, garlic and ketchup. Pour wine or water over the roast. Cover with foil wrap. Cook for one hour. Add carrots, onions and potatoes, cover and cook 30 minutes more. Uncover and roast for another half hour. Let stand 15 minutes before carving and serving.

SIRLOIN WITH MUSHROOMS

4 servings

1 2-pound sirloin steak, all fat removed	Salt and freshly ground pepper, to taste
$\frac{1}{4}$ cup teriyaki sauce (see page 113 for homemade teriyaki sauce)	1 teaspoon minced garlic
	$\frac{1}{2}$ pound sliced mushrooms
	$\frac{1}{2}$ cup beef broth

Preheat skillet to 400°.

Marinate steak in teriyaki sauce overnight, covered tightly or in a food storage bag. Add steak, reserving marinade. Sear for 5 minutes on each side. Add salt, pepper, garlic, mushrooms and simmer 2 minutes more. Add leftover marinade and broth. Heat until boiling and serve topped with additional black pepper, if desired.

Beef Pot Roast

12 servings

Here's a hearty dinner that's chock-full of low-fat goodness. Make this when you want to warm the soul and spirit!

8 cloves garlic
3 tablespoons wine
   vinegar
10 black peppercorns
1 tablespoon oregano

3 cups water
2 slices bacon, sliced
   crosswise into
1/4 -inch pieces
1 4-pound rump roast

Preheat oven to 325°.

Combine garlic, vinegar, peppercorns, oregano and water in a blender or food processor. Process until smooth, about one minute.

Heat bacon in a flame-proof casserole until it begins to smoke. Add the roast and brown all over. Pour garlic mixture over the roast and cover with foil. Bake for about 1 1/2 hours. Turn the meat over, baste with the sauce and cover again. Roast for another hour or until the meat is very tender when pierced with a fork.

Cool slightly and serve sliced thin with the sauce spooned over each piece.

Moist Meat Loaf

2–4 servings

A great microwave meal that's ready in minutes!

1 1/2 pounds lean ground
   round or chuck
2 tablespoons minced
   fresh garlic
2 medium onions,
   finely chopped
1/2 cup rolled oats

1 egg, beaten
2 tablespoons chopped
   fresh parsley
Salt and freshly ground pepper,
   to taste
1/4 cup ketchup

Place the meat on a 10-inch microwavable plate or casserole. Make a well in the center and add garlic, onions, oats, egg, parsley, salt and pepper. Pour in half the tomato sauce or all the ketchup. Mix well with your hands and form into an oval in the center of the dish. Pour the rest of the tomato sauce down the center.

Microwave, uncovered, on high for 16 minutes, rotating the dish twice. Microwave 5 minutes more on medium and let stand 5 minutes before serving. Cut into slices and serve with steamed broccoli or spinach and a green salad.

Roast Lamb

8 servings

A great roast that your family and guests will adore.

1 5-pound leg of lamb, trimmed of all visible fat	2 tablespoons dried oregano
5 cloves of garlic cut into slivers	$\frac{1}{4}$ cup lemon juice
	$\frac{1}{2}$ cup white wine

Preheat oven to 325°.

Wipe roast well with a damp paper towel and with a very sharp, small knife, cut about 20 holes into it. Insert a garlic sliver into each hole. Mix lemon juice and oregano and rub it over the lamb with your fingers. Place in a roasting pan and pour the wine into the pan. Cook, uncovered for about 1 $\frac{1}{2}$ hours, basting every 20 minutes with the pan juices. Let stand 15 minutes before carving.

SUCCULENT SKEWERS

4 servings

A wonderful dish for company or family.

1 pound top round, beef
   cut into 1-inch cubes
$^1/_2$ cup olive oil
$^1/_4$ cup red wine vinegar
2 cloves garlic, crushed
2 tomatoes, quartered

2 green peppers, cut
   into 1-inch chunks
1 large onion, quartered
   and separated
$^1/_2$ pound mushroom caps

Marinate the beef cubes in the dressing, combining the oil, vinegar and garlic overnight. Thread them onto metal skewers alternating with the vegetables. (I like to cover each beef cube with an onion piece, then a tomato, green pepper and mushroom cap.) Broil 5 inches from the heat source for 5 minutes each side or grill on an outdoor barbecue for the same length of time. Serve with rice.

PORK CHOPS

2 servings

This was one of the first dishes I ever made! It still is one of the tastiest, cheapest and simplest main-dish meals you can prepare.

2 tablespoons oil
4 pork chops, trimmed
   of visible fat
$^1/_2$ cup long-grain rice
2 cloves garlic, chopped
$^1/_4$ cup chopped onion

1$^1/_2$ cups chicken broth
1 green pepper, cored,
   seeded and chopped
1 tomato, sliced
Salt and freshly ground
pepper, to taste

Preheat an electric skillet to 350°. Add the oil.

Brown the pork chops for 5 minutes each side. Remove and place on a plate. Add rice, garlic and onions to the skillet. Stir until lightly brown, about 5 minutes. Add chicken broth and stir. Place the reserved pork chops over the rice mixture and top with green pepper and tomato slices. Cover skillet and cook for 20 minutes at 275° or until all liquid is absorbed.

ża   ża   ża   ża

MICROWAVED BARBECUED CHOPS

2 servings

Serve over rice with corn on the cob or a green vegetable. This is an easy after-work dish.

4 lean pork chops
½ cup barbecue sauce

1 onion, sliced
2 tablespoons minced fresh garlic

Place chops in a microwave-proof dish. Cover with sauce and top with sliced onion and garlic. Cover with vented plastic wrap and microwave on high for 5 minutes. Reduce power to medium and microwave 10 minutes longer.

APPLESAUCE ROAST PORK

5–6 servings

A wonderful company dinner!

1 3-pound pork rib roast
3 cloves garlic, minced
1 onion, sliced
1 teaspoon each oregano

1 cup unsweetened
  applesauce
2 teaspoons cinnamon
Salt and freshly ground pepper,
  to taste

Preheat oven to 350°.

Place pork roast in a pan. Cover with garlic, onion slices and spices. Let stand 4 hours, covered, before roasting. Roast, uncovered, for 1 hour. Let stand 15 minutes before carving. Serve with applesauce sprinkled with cinnamon.

HAM SCALLOP

4 servings

An easy microwave dish that makes tasty use of leftovers. You can add canned corn, sliced carrots or another favorite vegetable to the scallop for variation.

2 medium potatoes, sliced
1/2 onion, chopped
2 teaspoons minced garlic
8 thin slices ham
1 10-ounce can cream of celery soup
1/2 soup can skim milk
8 ounces grated mild Cheddar cheese
Salt and freshly ground pepper, to taste

Place the potato slices in a greased 2-quart baking dish in a neat layer or circular pattern. Cover with onion, minced garlic and ham slices. Mix soup with milk and pour over the casserole. Top with grated cheese and spices, to taste

Microwave, covered with vented plastic wrap, for 10 to 12 minutes on high or until potatoes are tender. Rotate dish halfway through cooking. Let stand before serving.

NOTE: You can also bake this dish covered with foil in a preheated 400 ° oven for 40 minutes.

BAKED HAM WITH PINEAPPLE

8–9 servings

A cooked ham will go a long way. Bake it on Sunday and you'll have leftovers for the week. Slice it for omelets and sandwiches. Or chop it to use in rice and pasta dishes.

Serve with roasted potatoes and Garlic Green Beans or Garlicky Carrots.

> 1 5-lb fully cooked ham, trimmed of all visible fat
> 15 whole cloves
> 3 cloves garlic, peeled
> 1 10-ounce can pineapple chunks or slices
> 1 small jar maraschino cherries for garnish, if desired

Preheat oven to 300°.

Place the ham in a roasting pan or baking dish. Cut the surface into diamond shapes with a sharp knife and place a whole clove in each intersection. Mince the garlic. Drain the pineapple slices and reserve the juice. Combine the garlic and juice and spoon over the ham. Place the pineapple over and around the ham. Roast, uncovered, for 1 hour, basting the ham with pan juices every 15 minutes or so. Remove to a platter to carve and surround with pineapple and cherries.

If garlic and poultry are a marriage made in gourmet heaven, then garlic teamed with fish must rank as the ultimate union!

Garlic Catfish Fillets

4 servings

Farm-raised catfish is healthful and almost pollution-free. These fillets are fast and easy to make.

2 pounds catfish fillets	2 tablespoons butter or
1 egg, beaten	margarine
1 tablespoon Worcestershire	4 cloves garlic, peeled
sauce	and left whole
1 cup cornmeal	Salt and freshly ground
pepper,	½ cup oil
to taste	

Dip fillets in the beaten egg mixed with Worcestershire sauce and dredge in cornmeal. Lay in a single layer on waxed paper. Meanwhile, heat the oil and butter in a large skillet. Add the cloves of garlic and stir to blend flavors. Add the fillets, one at a time. Brown for 3 minutes on each side or until the fish flakes easily with a fork. Serve with lemon wedges and sprinkle with white pepper.

Famous Greek Fish Fillets

4–6 servings

This easy and delicious recipe is sure to become a family favorite—even with those who say they hate fish. Serve the fillets over steamed brown rice and accompany with sliced Greek or Italian bread.

It's an ideal dish if you don't have access to a fish market. The tomato sauce cuts the "frozen" taste of the fish.

ès   ès   ès   ès

2 pounds fresh or frozen
   fish fillets
2 cloves garlic, chopped
1 medium onion, sliced
1 green pepper, cored,
   seeded and sliced
1 carrot, thinly sliced

2 cups tomato sauce
½ cup chicken broth or
   white wine
1 teaspoon oregano
1 teaspoon white pepper
¼ cup olive oil

Preheat oven to 350°.

Place fish fillets neatly along the bottom of a 9-x-13-inch pan. Cover evenly with vegetables and garlic. Blend tomato sauce with chicken broth or wine and pour over the fillets. Sprinkle with seasonings. Drizzle olive oil over the top. Bake, uncovered, for 30 minutes.

MOROCCAN CATFISH COUSCOUS

4–6 servings

We have learned to love couscous, a semolina cereal indigenous to Morocco and other North African countries. It's so easy to make. This recipe, from the Catfish Institute, makes excellent use of the grain.

¼ cup slivered almonds
2 tablespoons olive oil
1 medium onion, chopped
2 cloves garlic, minced
2 medium carrots, cut on
   the diagonal
1 small red pepper, cored,
   seeded and cut into strips
1 teaspoon ground
   coriander

2 cups chicken stock
4 Mississippi River catfish fillets
   cut into 2-inch strips
1 cup canned chickpeas,
   drained
1 medium zucchini, cut in
   half lengthwise then
   into 1-inch strips
1 cup couscous or rice

Toast almonds on a baking sheet in a 350° oven for 8 minutes. Heat oil in a large, heavy skillet and sauté onions, garlic, carrots, pepper and coriander.

Add chicken broth and 2 cups water. Bring to a boil and cook for 5 minutes. Add catfish, chickpeas and zucchini and simmer for 15 minutes. Prepare couscous or rice according to package directions and place on a large serving plate, making a well in the center.

Fill the well with the fish-vegetable mixture, reserving some of the broth and top with toasted almonds. Serve the cooking broth on the side.

EASY FISH CASSEROLE

4 servings

This stew-like casserole can be made with any available white fish fillet.

2 onions, sliced
2 pounds red potatoes, sliced
1 teaspoon butter
1 tablespoon olive oil
2 tablespoons minced garlic
3 tablespoons fresh parsley
1 cup low-sodium chicken
  broth

1 pound fish fillets
2 cups frozen peas, thawed
2 cloves garlic, peeled
  and minced
2 tablespoons oil
Salt and freshly ground pepper,
  to taste

Preheat oven to 350°.

Spread the onion and potato slices along the bottom of a greased 3-quart casserole. Sprinkle with butter, oil, garlic, parsley, salt and ground pepper. Add broth and bake, covered, for 30 minutes.

Arrange fish fillets on the potatoes. Add peas and garlic. Drizzle oil over the casserole and bake 15 minutes more. Uncover, season, and serve.

SHRIMP SCORPIO

3–4 servings

This is an excellent, easy dish. Serve it over fluffy white rice with a Greek salad. Add freshly baked Greek bread, a bottle of chilled, white Domestica wine (available in specialty shops) and you'll think you are dining in the Greek isles.

3 tablespoons olive oil
2 onions, minced
2 teaspoons garlic, minced
1/4 cup minced parsley
1 tablespoon finely
  minced dill
1/4 teaspoon dry mustard

2 cups fresh or canned
  peeled tomatoes, chopped
1/2 cup tomato sauce
1 pound large shrimp,
  peeled and deveined
1 cup crumbled feta cheese

Preheat oven to 425°.

Heat oil in a medium, 2-quart sauce pan and add onions. Cook, stirring, until the onion starts to brown. Add garlic, parsley, dill, mustard, tomatoes and tomato sauce. Simmer for 30 minutes. Add shrimp to sauce and cook for 3 minutes or until shrimp turns pink. Pour the mixture into a buttered, 2-quart casserole and sprinkle with crumbled cheese. Bake for 5 minutes, or until the cheese starts to melt. Serve immediately.

SAVORY SALMON STEAKS

2 servings

Put your microwave to work to make delicious and tender salmon steaks. Serve them with steamed rice and a green vegetable.

2 salmon steaks, cut 1-inch thick
1/4 cup honey mustard or ranch dressing
1 teaspoon each pepper and dill
2 teaspoons minced fresh garlic

Place salmon steaks in a shallow microwavable dish. Top with dressing, spices and garlic. Cover with vented plastic wrap. Microwave on high for 8 minutes. Let stand 3 minutes before serving.

SUPER SCALLOPS

2–3 servings

A quick and easy dish that's great with a side order of spaghetti cooked and tossed with butter and garlic and steamed broccoli!

2 teaspoons butter or
  margarine
1 cup chopped scallions
2 cloves garlic, chopped
1 pound sea scallops

$^1/_2$ cup chicken broth
  or white wine
1 teaspoon dill
Lemon wedges, for garnish

Heat butter in a frying pan. Add scallops, scallions and garlic. Sauté on medium heat for 5 minutes. Pour in broth or wine and simmer, uncovered, for 5 more minutes. Sprinkle dill over the scallops and serve with lemon wedges.

Garlic is a most versatile seasoning that lends itself to a wide array of foods—from all-purpose Garlic Butter to unusual Garlic Chip Cookies.

GARLIC BUTTER

Makes ³/₄ cup

It pays to have ready-made garlic butter on hand to slather over fresh bread, toast, meats, vegetables or pasta—anything that could use a dash of zippy flavor. It keeps for weeks in the refrigerator.

½ cup butter or margarine
3 cloves fresh garlic, finely minced

Mix butter by hand or with an electric mixer until creamy smooth. Add garlic and blend well. Store, covered, in the refrigerator or freezer for later use.

NOTE: You can increase the amount of garlic if you are a real aficionado. I use up to 6 cloves!

GARLIC MARINADE

Makes 1 cup

This aromatic marinade is superb on meat, fish, steaks, shellfish or poultry.

³/₄ cup olive oil
3 cloves garlic, crushed
¼ cup wine vinegar
1 teaspoon oregano

Salt and freshly ground pepper, to taste
1 teaspoon Worcestershire sauce

Mix all the ingredients well in a jar. Store in the refrigerator.

VARIATION #1: To add a real barbecue flavor for chicken or ribs, mix in ¼ cup ketchup and ¼ cup soy sauce.

VARIATION #2: For a sweeter marinade, ideal for chicken breasts, add ¼ cup honey and 2 tablespoons Dijon-style mustard.

ൠ   ൠ   ൠ   ൠ

Seasoning Salt

Makes ¹/₂ cup

Feel free to adapt this basic recipe to include your own favorite spices.

2 tablespoons garlic salt	¹/₄ teaspoon thyme
2 tablespoons white pepper	¹/₄ teaspoon chili powder
2 tablespoons dried oregano	¹/₄ teaspoon curry powder
¹/₄ teaspoon paprika	6 cloves garlic, peeled

Blend well and store in a shaker-top jar, tightly covered, in a cool place.

Teriyaki Sauce

Makes 1 quart

You can make your own tasty, Oriental-style sauce at home. This keeps for months and is great on poultry, fish or game.

2 cups soy or tamari sauce	¹/₄ cup rice wine vinegar
¹/₄ cup honey	¹/₄ cup dry sherry
2 tablespoons lemon juice	1 piece fresh ginger (2-inch)
	6 cloves garlic, peeled

Combine all ingredients in a blender. Store in a glass jar in the refrigerator.

Vegetable Relish

Makes 4 cups

This tasty recipe makes an ideal hostess gift.

4 medium carrots
2 medium onions
1 medium green pepper
1 cup chopped cabbage
1 cup green beans
1 cup wax beans

4 cloves garlic
2 cups sugar
2 cups cider or
    balsamic vinegar
2 tablespoons each celery and
    mustard seeds

Cut up all vegetables. Place about 2 cups of them at a time in the blender. Cover with water. Add garlic. Process until coarsely chopped. Drain. Pour into a glass bowl or crock and cover with salted water.

Let stand at least 8 hours. Drain thoroughly, pressing out excess liquid. Mix vinegar, sugar, celery seed and mustard seed in a large saucepan. Heat to boiling. Stir in vegetables, reduce heat and simmer, uncovered for 10 more minutes.

Pack into hot jars, leaving 1/4-inch head room. Seal well and process in boiling water for 10 minutes to sterilize.

Garlic Dill Pickles

Makes 6 quarts

There is nothing like the taste of homemade, garlic pickles! Do give these a try.

36–40 pickling cukes
    (the smaller, the better)
7 1/2 cups water
5 cups white vinegar
1/2 cup pickling or
    non-iodized salt

12 cloves garlic, sliced
6 sprigs fresh dill
6 tablespoons dill seed
6 slices onion

Wash and scrub cukes carefully, cutting a quarter-inch slice from the blossom end of each one. Heat water, vinegar and salt to the boiling point in a large Dutch oven. Place 2 cloves of garlic, 1 sprig of dill, 1 tablespoon dill seed and 1 onion slice into each of 6 hot jars. Pack cukes neatly into the jars, allowing 1/2-inch head room. Cover with boiling brine. Seal and process in a boiling water bath to sterilize for 10 minutes.

SKORDALIA

Makes 3 cups

This traditional Greek recipe bases its unique flavor on the unusual combination of mashed potatoes and garlic. It can be served as an appetizer or as an ideal accompaniment to a festive dinner. It's one of my parents' favorite recipes and one that I am proud to pass on.

6 medium potatoes, peeled, boiled and mashed	$1/2$ cup lemon juice or white vinegar
4 cloves garlic, crushed	3 egg yolks
1 cup olive oil	

Add hot mashed potatoes and garlic to the large bowl of an electric mixer. Beat well. Alternate slowly adding the oil and lemon juice or vinegar. When the ingredients are thoroughly mixed, beat in the egg yolks to make the mixture fluffy. Chill before serving.

THE BEST PIZZA DOUGH

By making pizza at home, you get to add as much of your favorite toppings as you want! We usually make a large pizza, on a specially made pan with vent holes that allow for even cooking, and divide it in half—one side for my husband's meats and one side for my veggies.

But the real reason to make homemade pizza is so that you can add lots of garlic right into the crust!

1 cup warm water	2 tablespoons garlic powder
1 package rapid-rise yeast	1 tablespoon oregano
1 teaspoon sugar	3 cups flour, a mixture of all-purpose and whole wheat works well
1 teaspoon salt	
$1/4$ cup oil	

☙ ☙ ☙ ☙

Dissolve yeast and sugar in warm water in a large bowl; let it stand until it starts to bubble. In the meantime, assemble the other ingredients.

Mix salt, oil, spices and 1 cup flour into the dissolved yeast. Beat well. Add remaining flour, $1/2$ cup at a time, beating well with a wooden spoon. When you have a very stiff dough, use your hands to mix in just enough of the remaining flour so that your dough is no longer sticky. Knead 20 turns and place dough into a warm, oiled bowl. Cover with a damp towel or plastic wrap. Let it rise in a warm place for 30 minutes. Punch down the dough and pat onto a greased pizza pan. Let rise again for 20 minutes.

Top with your favorite, garlicky tomato sauce and choice of toppings. Place in a *cold* oven, on the lowest rack, and turn the heat to 500°. Bake for 20 minutes or until nicely browned.

GARLIC CHIP COOKIES

Makes 5 dozen

I've included these unusual cookies just to prove that garlic has a place in any course of any meal! Even the little cookie monsters in your household will adore these healthy treats.

10 cloves garlic	2 cups chocolate or
$1/2$ cup honey	butterscotch chips
1 cup butter, softened	$1/2$ cup chopped nuts
1 cup brown sugar	$2 1/2$ cups flour
2 eggs	1 teaspoon baking soda
1 teaspoon vanilla	1 teaspoon salt

Preheat oven to 375°.

Drop garlic cloves into boiling water for 5 minutes. Then peel, chop and soak them in the honey for 20 minutes. Cream butter, sugar, eggs and vanilla.

Combine flour, baking soda and salt. Add to creamed mixture. Stir in chips and nuts. Drain garlic and add to batter. Blend well. Form cookies by dropping heaping tablespoons of batter onto an ungreased baking sheet, about 2 inches apart.

Bake until lightly browned. Remove from pan and cool on racks.

❧   ❧   ❧   ❧

GARLIC ICE CREAM

Makes 1 quart

1 to 1 ½ teaspoons gelatin
¼ cup cold water
2 cups milk
¾ to 1 cup sugar

⅛ teaspoon salt
2 tablespoons lemon juice
2 cloves garlic, minced
2 cups whipping cream

Soak the gelatin in cold water. Bring the milk, sugar and salt to a boil. Dissolve the gelatin in the hot milk. Cool, then add the lemon juice and garlic. Chill the mixture until slushy. Whip the cream until thick but not stiff and fold into the mixture. Freeze in a mold, or in a foil-covered tray.

NOTE: A fruit topping works well with this dessert.

GARLIC JELLY

½ cup fresh garlic,
  finely chopped
2 cups white wine vinegar
5 ½ cups sugar
3 cups water

1 2-ounce package
  powdered pectin
¼ teaspoon butter or oil
2 drops food coloring
(optional)

Combine the garlic and vinegar in a 2- to 2½-quart kettle. Simmer the mixture gently, uncovered, over medium heat for 15 minutes. Remove the pan from the heat and pour the mixture into a 1-quart glass jar. Cover and let it stand at room temperature for 24 to 36 hours.

Pour the flavored vinegar through a wire strainer into a bowl, pressing the garlic with the back of a spoon to squeeze out as much liquid as possible. Discard any residue. Measure the liquid and add vinegar, if needed, to make 1 cup.

Measure the sugar into a dry bowl. Combine the garlic-vinegar solution and the water in a 5- or 6-quart kettle. Add the package of powdered pectin to the liquids in the kettle, stirring it in well.

Over high heat, bring the mixture to a boil, stirring it constantly to avoid scorching. Add the premeasured sugar, and stir it in well. Bring the mixture to a full rolling boil (a boil that cannot be stirred down). Add the ¼ teaspoon butter to reduce foaming. Continue stirring. Boil the mixture hard exactly 2 minutes.

Remove the pan from the heat. Skim any foam. Add red, yellow or orange food coloring, if desired. Pour the jelly into prepared glasses. Seal according to directions on recipe folder in pectin package.

SPOT'S STEW

This recipe is from Andi Brown of Tampa, Florida. Andi makes enough food to feed her kitty, Spot, for about a month. You can use the same formula for dogs, too.

2 onions, chopped	1 cup broccoli, chopped
¾ head of garlic—that's the whole head, not just a clove!	4 carrots
	1 whole zucchini
	1 whole yellow squash
1 whole fryer chicken	1 handful green beans
1 pound brown rice	2 stalks celery

In a 10-quart stainless steel stock pot, put 3 tablespoons oil. Heat the oil and brown onions and garlic lightly. Add chicken and fill the pot with water.

Simmer for three hours. Let cool and debone the chicken. Using an electric mixer, whip the ingredients into a puree. Put portions into zip-lock bags and store in the freezer.

How to Age Garlic

This recipe is contributed by Allen Beygi of the Health & Life store in Escondido, California. Use at your discretion as a tonic or to flavor your favorite garlic recipes.

5 pounds fresh garlic
$\frac{1}{2}$ gallon distilled white vinegar
Waxed paper

4–5 tablespoons salt
1 gallon-sized glass jar with a plastic lid

1. Sterilize a 1 gallon-sized glass jar.
2. Cut off bottom club (root area) of each garlic bunch.
3. Remove garlic husks (skin). Leave on the last skin area, vinegar will soften it.
4. Add 4–5 tablespoons salt to vinegar.
5. Bring $\frac{1}{2}$ gallon vinegar (with salt added) to a boil.
6. Put garlic in glass jar.
7. *Very slowly* add vinegar to garlic in glass jar so the jar will not crack.
8. Wait $\frac{1}{2}$ hour and put a piece of waxed paper on top of jar and then put on the plastic lid tightly.
9. Put the date on the top of the jar.
10. One week later, add more vinegar. (If you have leftover cold vinegar, you may use this.)
11. It is not necessary to store garlic in the refrigerator.
12. Store on the shelf for a minimum time of 6 months; 1 year to 2 years is much better. Perfect after 3 years.

TIPS
Organic purple garlic is the best.
Garlic will turn purple over time and vinegar turns "syrupy" and is delicious!

Index

❢ ❢ ❢ ❢

&a &a &a &a

All CC
direct
Depa

Nev

How
Natio
Creat
Life &
Unfir
Lynn
1001
The N
Natu
Unco
Hit o
Worl

Bac

Thinl
Com
Creat

Dr. Cookie's Cookbook (comb) .... 1-56790-109-3 .... $7.95
Dr. Cookie's Cookbook (Paper) .... 1-56790-108-5 .... $6.95
Early American Cookbook .... 1-56790-087-9 .... $7.95
Essential Book of Shellfish .... 1-56790-125-5 .... $6.95
How to Be a Wine Expert .... 1-9613525-1-5 .... $9.95
Muffin Mania .... 1-56790-074-7 .... $7.95
One Day Celestial Navigation........................ 1-56790-021-6 .... $9.95

Sub-total

Please add $2.00 for postage and handling

Florida residents add 6% sales tax to order.

TOTAL

Bill To: _____

_____

_____

_____

_____

Ship To: _____

_____

_____

_____

_____

"I hope this book has enhanced your life. I promise that any or all of my books can make your life better! - Lynn Allison

TO ORDER MORE OF LYNN'S BOOKS

Send a check or money order to:

BETTER LIFESTYLE SERIES
7210 CARMEL COURT
BOCA RATON FLORIDA 33433

*Natural Stressbusters for the Whole Family ($7.95) --------------------------
*The Magic of Garlic: Nature's Number One Healing Food ($7.95) --------------
*1,001 Ways to Make Your Life Better ($7.95) --------------------------------
Include $2.50 Shipping and handling per book. ------------------------------

Total: _____

Delivery between 6-8 weeks. Make sure that you include a printed return address and a day time telephone number. Many thanks!

Don't miss out on these best-selling titles by Lynn Allison!

1001 Ways to Make Your Life Better
Included are quick and easy ways to reduce stress, increase your brain power, improve your family life and take control of your destiny, plus many more. We all want to get our lives organized, maintain our health and stay young at heart. Now we can—simply by opening this book to any page.

The Magic of Garlic
Researchers say garlic wards off cancer and heart disease and keeps the blood healthy by preventing clots; it acts as an antibiotic in fighting colds, and it can even keep fleas off the family dog. *The Magic of Garlic* presents the practical applications of this marvelous herb, along with a historical overview and delicious recipes you can use to get more garlic into your daily diet.

Natural Stress-Busters
Stress is a major health problem in this country today, but it is manageable. Lynn Allison reveals how anyone of any age can enjoy a positive, stress-free life by taking advantage of the tools nature has provided for that purpose. In addition to tests to determine stress levels and exercises designed to reduce tension, *Natural Stress-Busters* even includes a two-week diary you can use to measure your progress.

Stress-Busting Meditations
Contains 40 minutes of soothing pre-recorded meditations designed to help you reduce stress and tension. Includes the blissful sounds of nature in the background.

1001 Ways to Make Your Life Better.................1-56790-097-6 ....$7.95	_____
The Magic of Garlic ....1-56790-098-4 ....$7.95	_____
Natural Stress-Busters.................................1-56790-099-2 ....$7.95	_____
Stress-Busting Meditations...$9.95	_____

Sub-total   _____

Please add $2.00 for postage and handling   _____

Florida residents add 6% sales tax to order.   _____

TOTAL   _____

Bill To: _____

_____

_____

_____

Ship To:_____

_____

_____

_____